CW01023990

The Young Phonographer V1: And Shorthand Beginner's Magazine

Oliver McEwan

THIRD EDITION.

All Trade Orders through Mr. JOHN HEYWOOD, 2, Amen Corner, E.C.; and Deansgate, Manchester.

THE

Young Phonographer,

— AND —

SHORTHAND BEGINNER'S MAGAZINE.

EDITED BY OLIVER McEWAN,

EDITOR "McEWAN'S PHONOGRAPHIC MAGAZINE," "THE SHORTHAND CRITIC AND REVIEW," AND "SHORTHAND NOTES AND QUERIES."

No. 1. VOL. I.] NOVEMBER, 1893. [Price 1d., 1/6 per annum, post free.

IMPORTANT.

INSTRUCTIONS FOR READING THIS MAGAZINE.

THE chief difference between the Shorthand in this Magazine and that in *McEwan's Phonographic Magazine* is that in *M.P.M. Phraseography* is employed; in the *Y.P.* the only phrases used are those found in the list of Grammalogues. Yet, though the briefest outlines and contractions are used, this Magazine may be read by those who possess the *most elementary* knowledge of Phonography if they will strictly observe the following instructions:—

1. All outlines *not vocalised* are *grammalogues*, and will be found on pages 92-5 or 198-9 of "Instructor."* The reader should, as soon as possible, commit to memory the grammalogues by writing them over and over again. In the meantime, when the reader comes across an *unvocalised* outline which he cannot read, should search for it amongst the grammalogues. This frequent reference will be decidedly beneficial to the student.

2. All outlines marked * are *contractions*, and will be found either in pages 101-2 or 142-5 of the "Instructor,"* to which reference should be always made when a character marked * is not known.

3. All words other than grammalogues and con-contractions are vocalised.

4. It is assumed that the reader is well acquainted with the consonants and vowels, and that he has also studied the Text Books so far as they include all *hooks, circles* and *loops*, and the halving principle.

5. All outlines which are formed in accordance with principles of abbreviation other than those noticed in the preceding paragraph, are indicated by the close proximity of figures. Those figures represent the number of the rule in the "Instructor" which explains the outline, and which should at once be referred to and studied if the outline is unknown.

6. Begin to read the Magazine from the *first* page—do not *dip* here and there.

7. By rigidly carrying out the instructions I have given above, the student will make advances in reading and in knowledge that will be surprising to him.

O. McE.

*"*The Grammalogues and Contractions*" are separately published at 2d. by the Messrs. Pitman.

EDITORIAL.

OUR INTENTIONS.

Free Assistance.

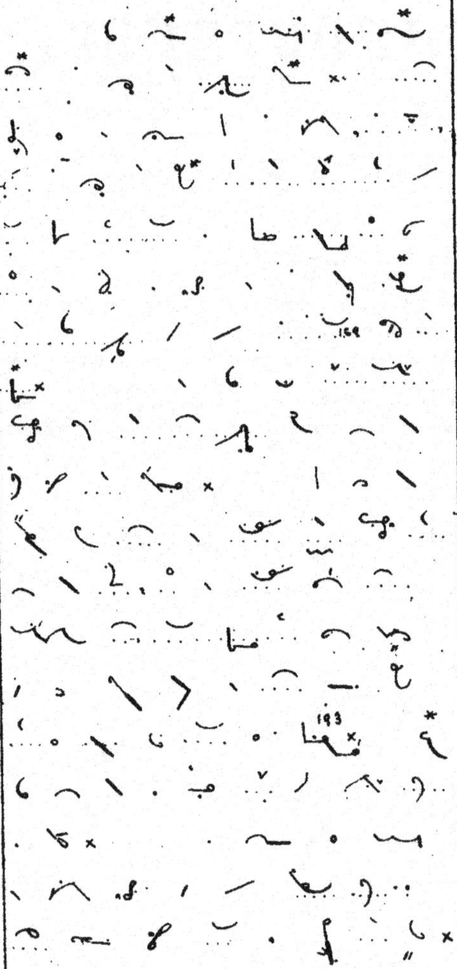

The Editor—A Teacher.

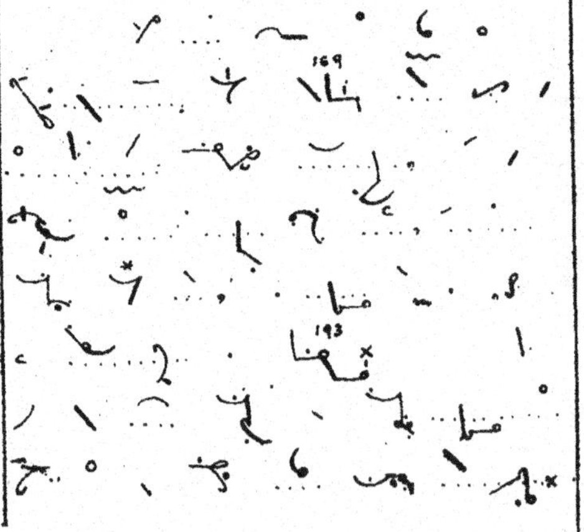

Teachers may Help.

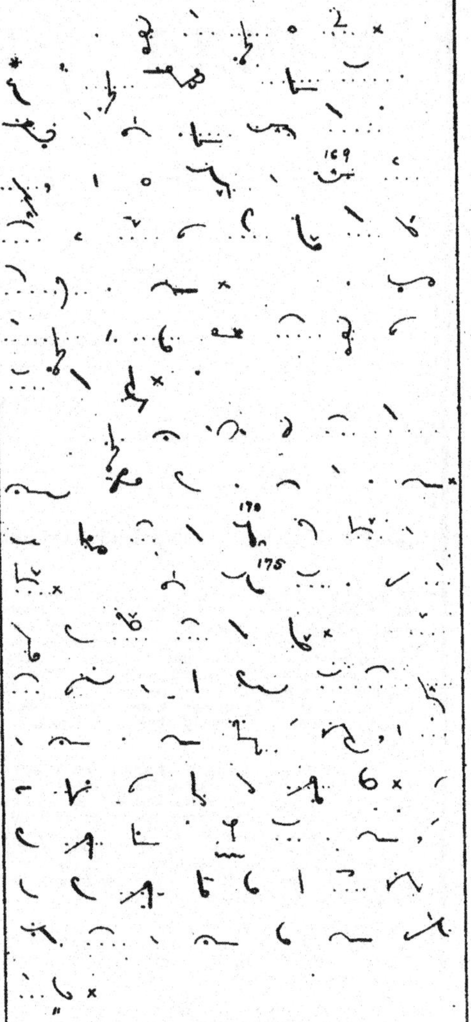

Be Vigilant.

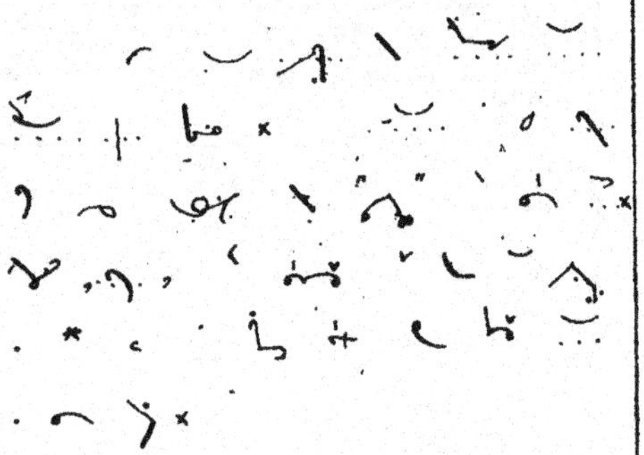

Oliver McEwan.

HELPS

TO THE STUDY OF PHONOGRAPHY.

By the Editor.

One Method of Study.

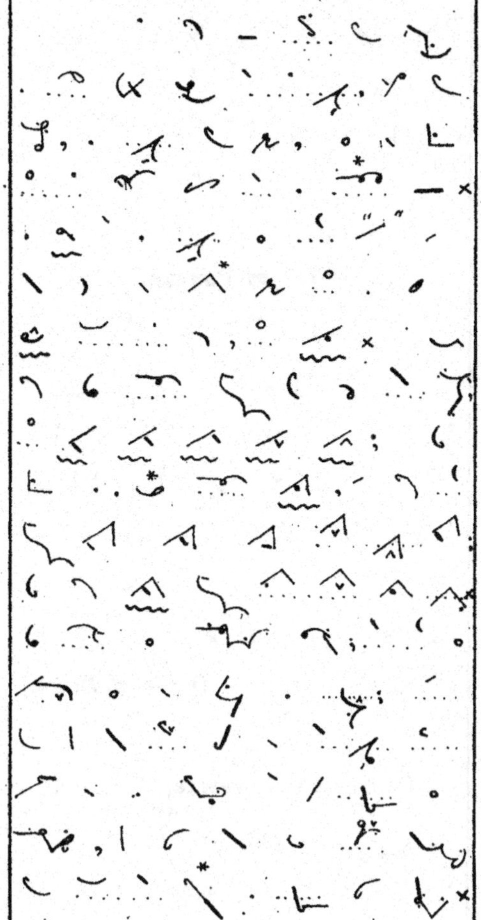

Daily Practice.

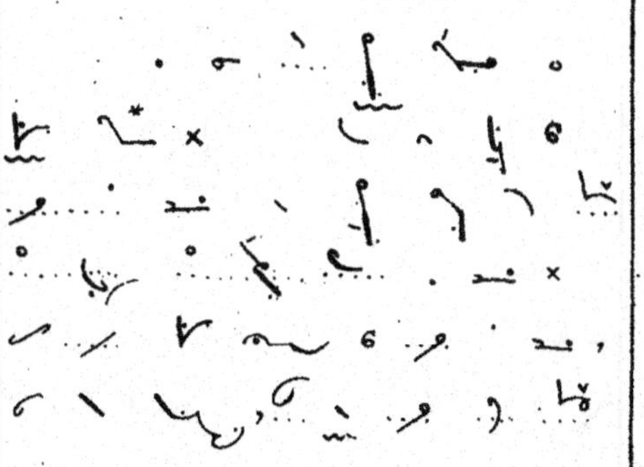

Neatness Essential.

Neatly.

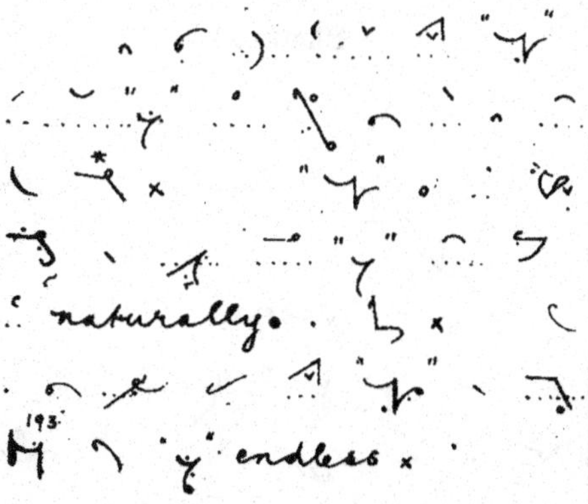

"Ly."

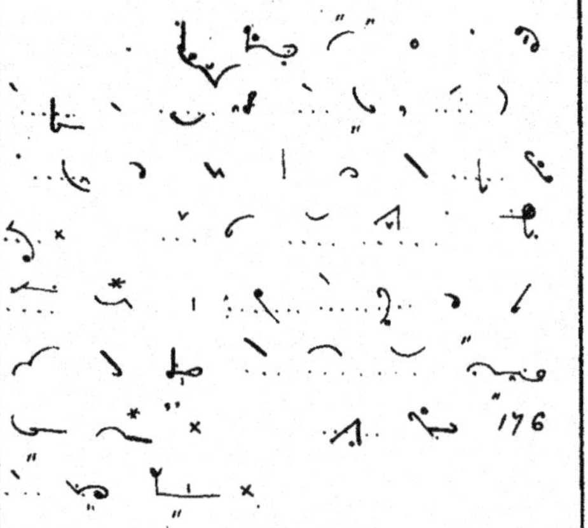

Slovenly.

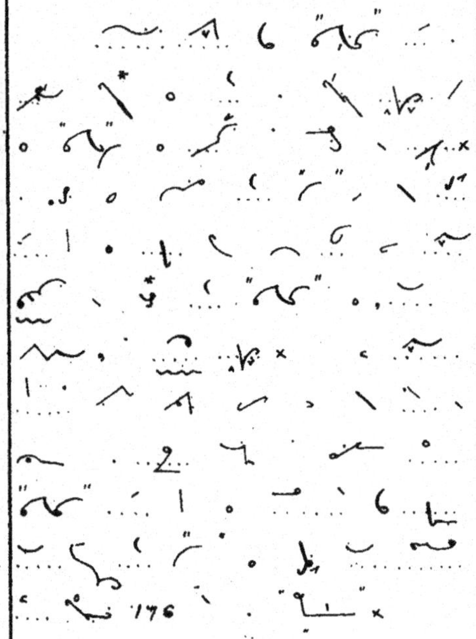

Plainly.

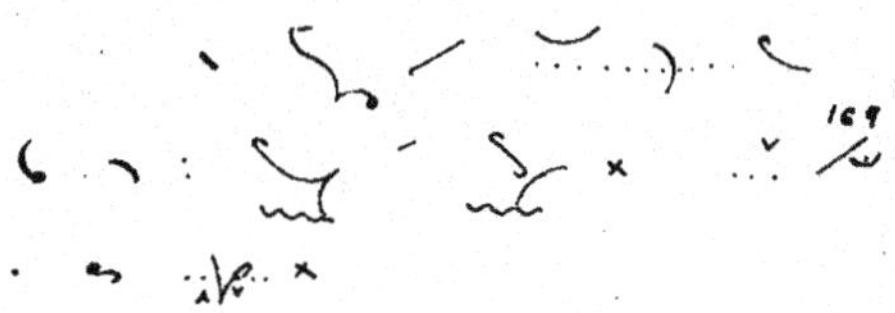

Deeply.

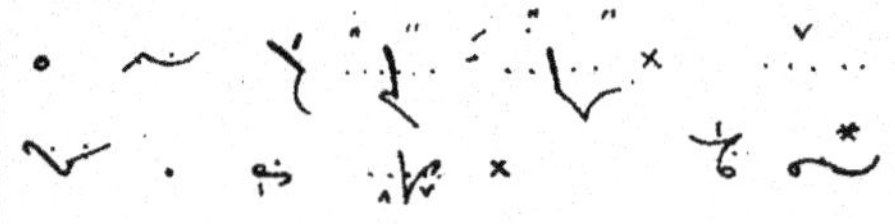

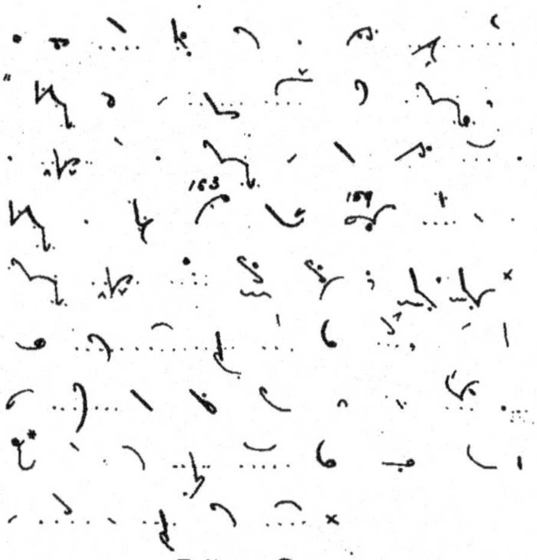

"L" in Puzzle.

Oliver McEwan.

Confusing Downward R and L.

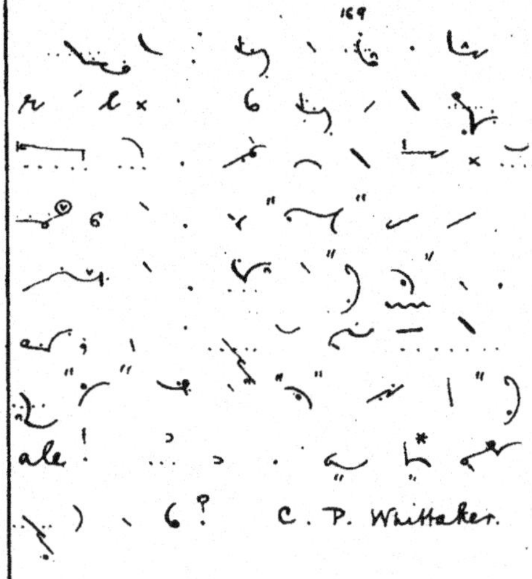

C. P. Whittaker.

THE GRAMMALOGUES AND ALL ABOUT THEM.

By the Editor.

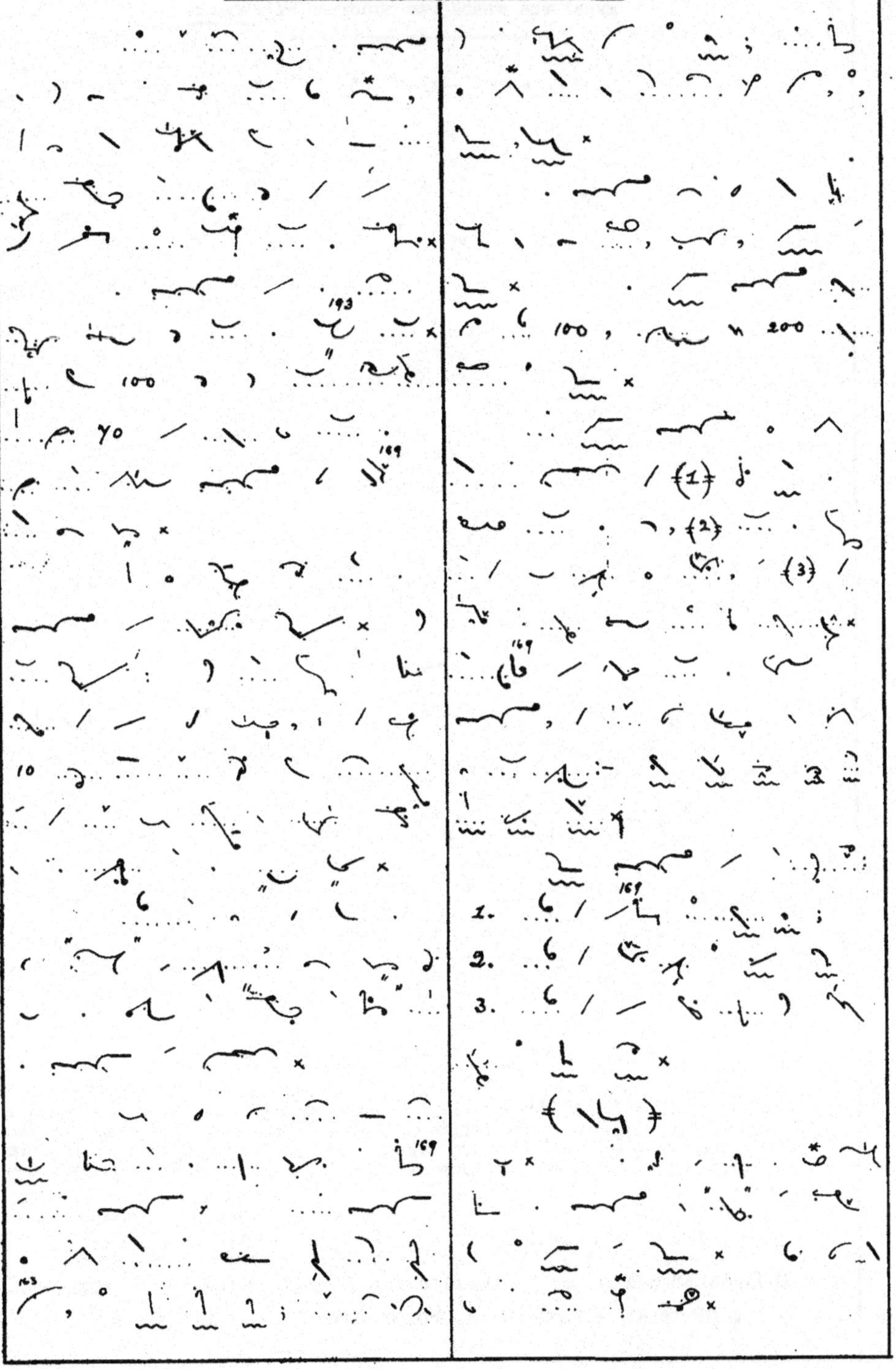

FOR DICTATION.

A SPEECH OF THE LATE JOHN BRIGHT.

EVERY TEN WORDS ARE INDICATED BY A SPACE.

THE TEACHERS.

Every Teacher of Phonography whose name and address is available will receive a free copy of No. 1 of *The Young Phonographer*. As the Magazine is intended to help Teachers in their work by giving to pupils an additional interest in the study of Phonography, the Editor very earnestly seeks the aid of his brother Teachers in making the Magazine known amongst students. Special terms as follows are offered to those who will take quantities:—

1 Month.	PREPAID. 3 Months.	6 Months.	12 Months.
8 Copies, 6d., post free.	1/6	3/-	6/-
13 " " "	2/3	4/6	9/-

Half-price allowed for unsold copies at the end of year, *when renewing subscription.*

EDITORIAL ADDRESS: 4, FURNIVALS INN, LONDON, E.C.

McEWAN'S PHONOGRAPHIC MAGAZINE,

16 PAGES. 4D. MONTHLY; 4/6 PER ANNUM.

TWO GRAND COMPETITIONS:

☞ £100

IN SEVEN HUNDRED PRIZES.

Competition No. 1.

For Teachers, Secretaries of S.W.A., and Agents for the Magazine.

Anyone who can get New Readers may enter.

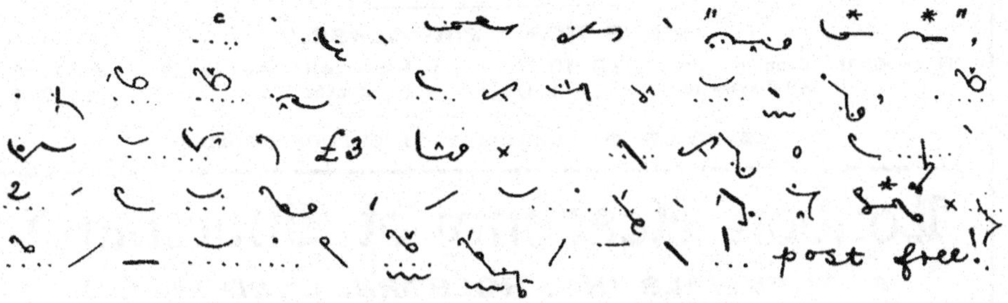

PRIZE LIST: COMPETITION No. 1.

One First Prize of **£3** cash.
Two Second Prizes of **£1** cash.
Seven Third Prizes, value **10/6** (Swan Fountain Pens).
Twelve Fourth Prizes, value **6/6** (Bound Vols. *McEwan's Phon. Mag.)*
Fifty Fifth Prizes, value **5/-** (Bound Vols. *Shorthand Notes and Queries*).
One Hundred Sixth Prizes, value **3/-** (Unbound *Ditto*).
Two Hundred Seventh Prizes, value **1/-** (Unbound Vols. *Critic and Review*).

COMPETITION No. 2—For Annual Subscribers.
Same Prize List as in Competition No. 1.

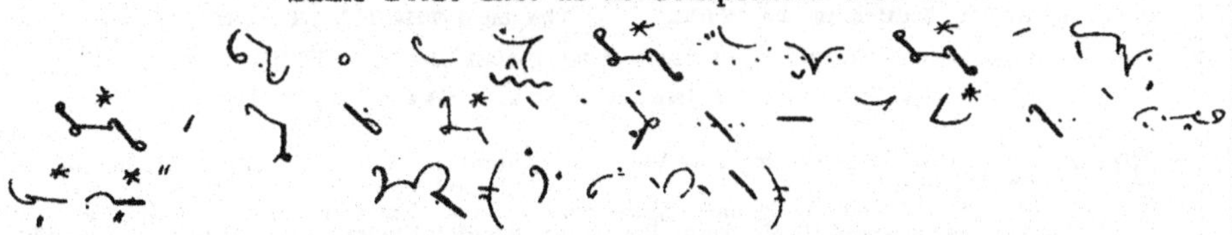

1000 Special Certificates of Merit.

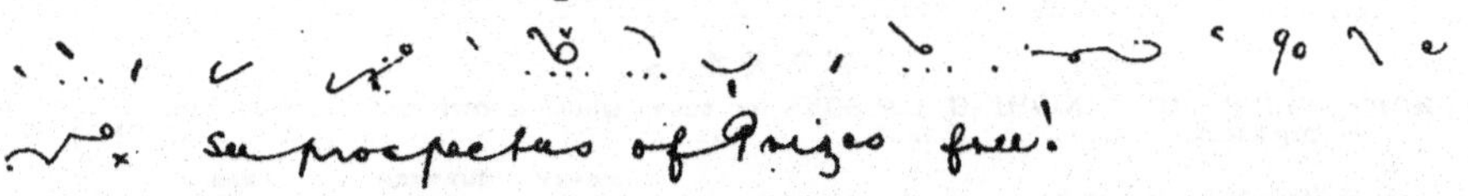

During 1894, 60 "Swan" Fountain Pens will be offered for Competition.

Send for Prize Prospectus and Specimen Copy (free) of "McEwan's Phonographic Magazine."

EDITORIAL ADDRESS: 4, FURNIVALS INN, HOLBORN, LONDON.

SEE GRAND COMPETITION (BACK PAGE), MEDALS, PRIZES AND CERTIFICATES.

THE

Young Phonographer,

— AND —

SHORTHAND BEGINNER'S MAGAZINE.

EDITED BY OLIVER McEWAN,

EDITOR "McEWAN'S PHONOGRAPHIC MAGAZINE," "THE SHORTHAND CRITIC AND REVIEW," AND "SHORTHAND NOTES AND QUERIES."

No. 2. VOL. I.] DECEMBER, 1893. [Price 1d.. 1/6 per annum, post free.

HELPS TO THE STUDY.

BY THE EDITOR.

THOUGHT.

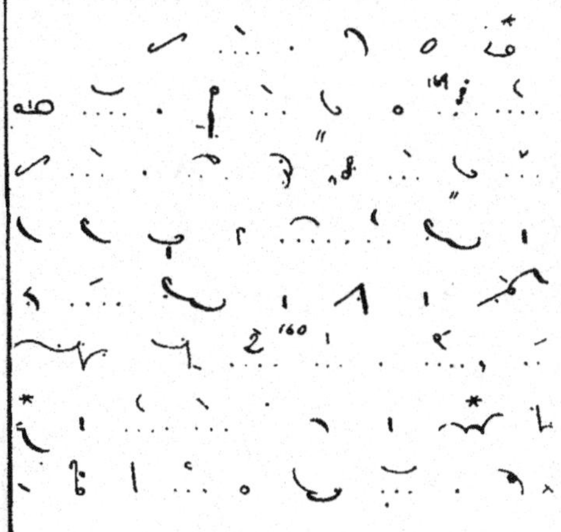

THOUGHT PRACTICE.

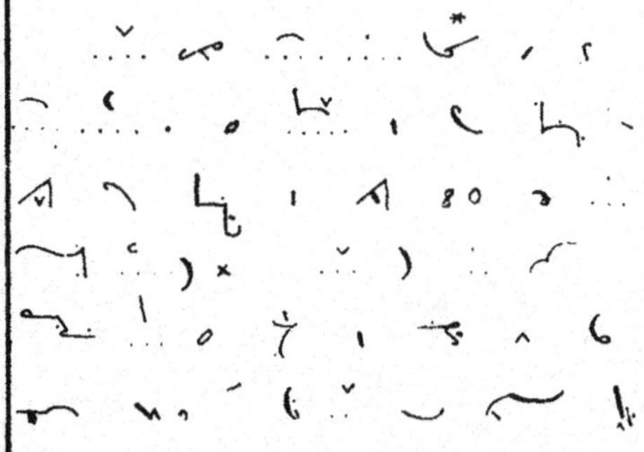

Mental and Physical Exercise.

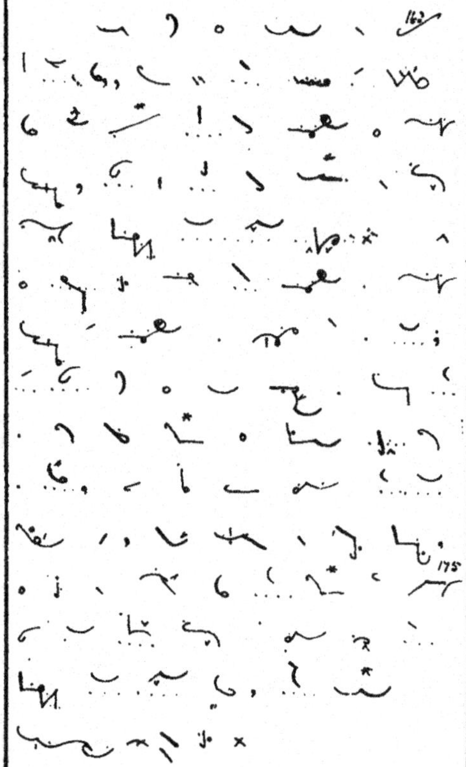

How to Prepare for Exams.

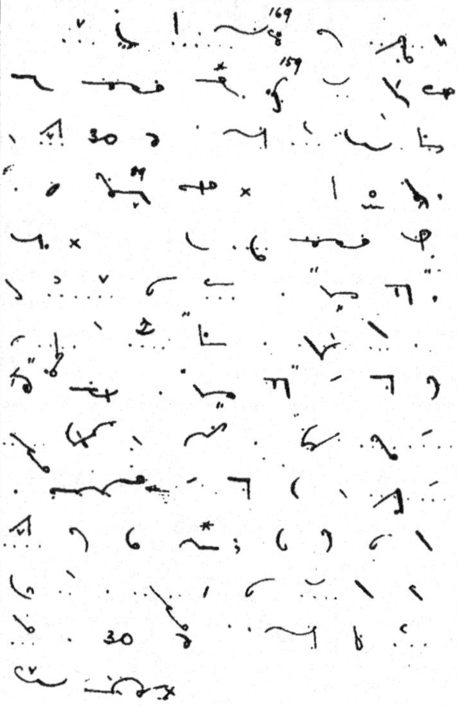

The Whitehall Review says:—"A new Magazine, entitled *The Young Phonographer and Shorthand Beginner's Magazine*, has just seen the light, and bids fair to supply a long-felt want. It is published at one penny monthly, and the editor is Mr. Oliver McEwan, who has, during this year, issued no fewer than four Phonographic Magazines. As its name implies, it is intended for beginners. The first number contains an article 'Helps to the Study of Phonography,' wherein the editor gives valuable advice to young students; 'The Grammalogues, and all about Them,' a special article by the editor; and a speech of John Bright, prepared for the purpose of dictation. The novice in Shorthand will be able to read this new Magazine. Contractions are indicated by an asterisk; grammalogues are recognised by the absence of vowels; and all other characters are fully vocalised. In the instances where advanced principles have been introduced, reference numbers are given to the rules in the Pitman Text Book, in accordance with which they are formed. Mr. John Heywood, Manchester and London, is the publisher."

Over 1,200 newspapers have given similar notices.

THE GRAMMALOGUES AND ALL ABOUT THEM.

By the Editor.

(Continued from last Month).

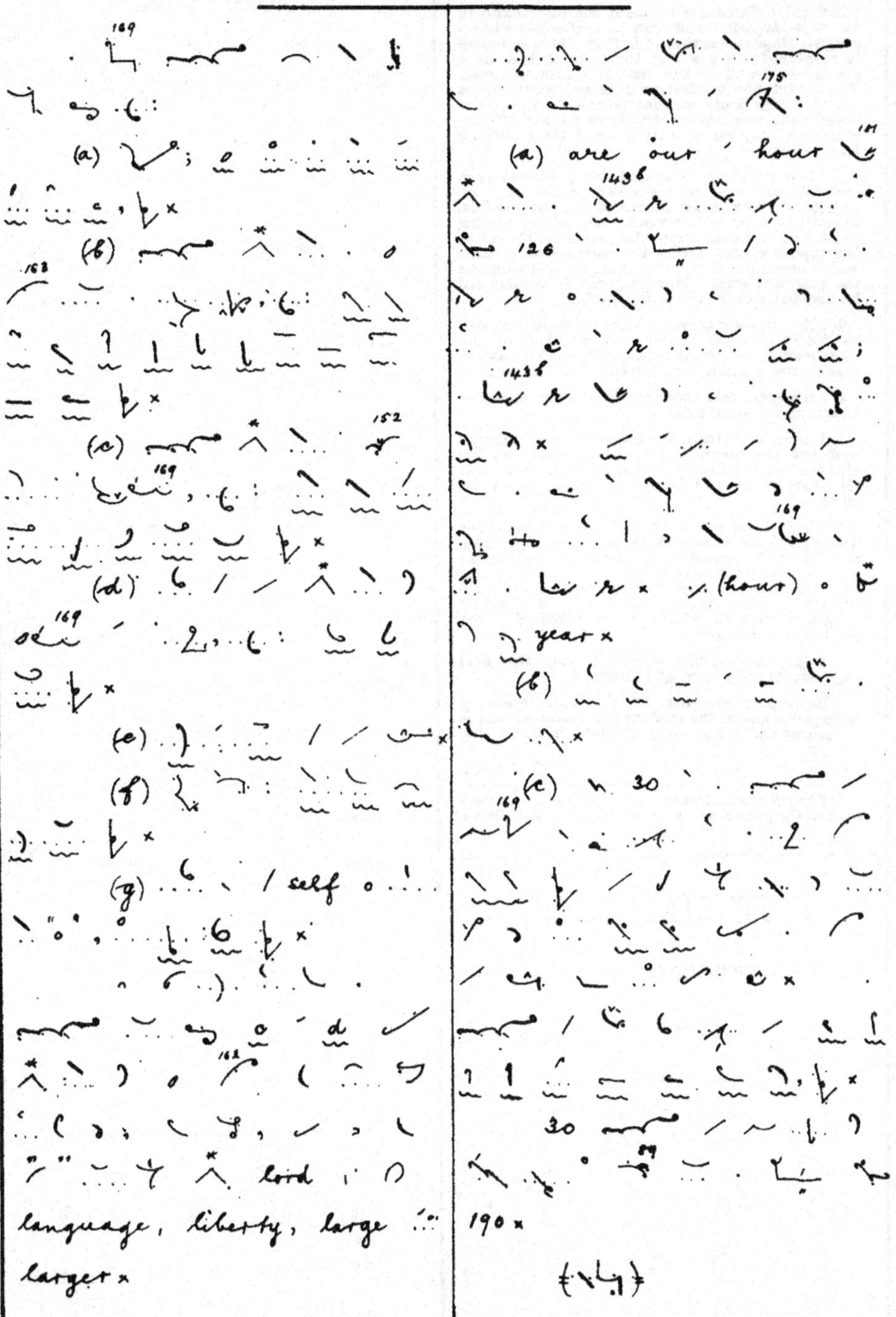
are our hour
(hour)
year
self
lord
language, liberty, large
larger
190

IMPORTANT.

INSTRUCTIONS FOR READING THIS MAGAZINE.

The chief difference between the Shorthand in this Magazine and that in *McEwan's Phonographic Magazine* is that in *M.P.M. Phraseography* is employed; in the *Y.P.* the only phrases used are those found in the list of Grammalogues. Yet, though the briefest outlines and contractions are used, this Magazine may be read by those who possess the *most elementary* knowledge of Phonography if they will strictly observe the following instructions:—

1. All outlines *not vocalised* are *grammalogues*, and will be found on pages 92-5 or 128-9 of "Instructor."* The reader should, as soon as possible, commit to memory the grammalogues by writing them over and over again. In the meantime, when the reader comes across an *unvocalised* outline which he cannot read, should search for it amongst the grammalogues. This frequent reference will be decidedly beneficial to the student.

2. All outlines marked * are *contractions*, and will be found either in pages 101-2 or 142-5 of the "Instructor,"* to which reference should be always made when a character marked * is not known.

3. All words other than grammalogues and contractions are vocalised.

4. It is assumed that the reader is well acquainted with the consonants and vowels, and that he has also studied the Text Books so far as they include all *hooks*, *circles* and *loops*, and the halving principle.

5. All outlines which are formed in accordance with principles of abbreviation other than those noticed in the preceding paragraph, are indicated by the close proximity of figures. Those figures represent the number of the rule in the "Instructor" which explains the outline, and which should at once be referred to and studied if the outline is unknown.

6. Begin to read the Magazine from the *first* page—do not *dip* here and there.

7. By rigidly carrying out the instructions I have given above, the student will make advances in reading and in knowledge that will be surprising to him.

O. McE.

*"*The Grammalogues and Contractions*" *are separately published at 2d. by the Messrs. Pitman.*

EDITORIAL NOTES.

An Unprecedented Success.

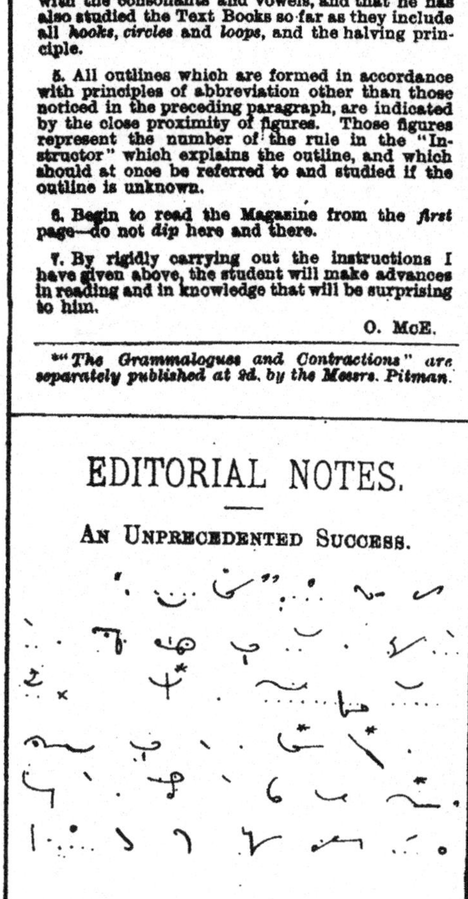

9,000 Copies.

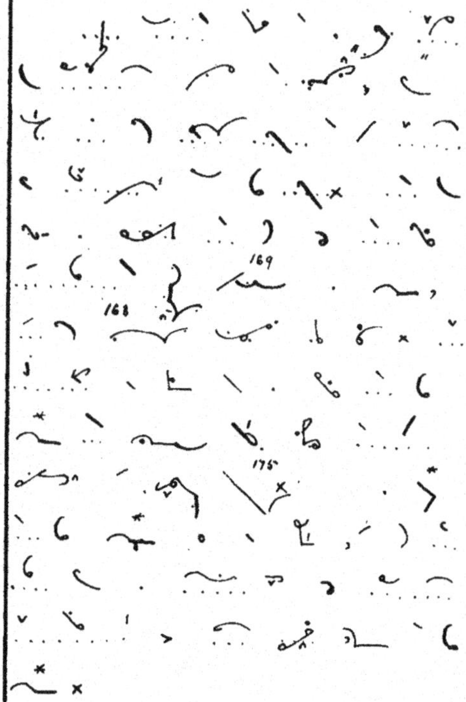

Neatness Examination.

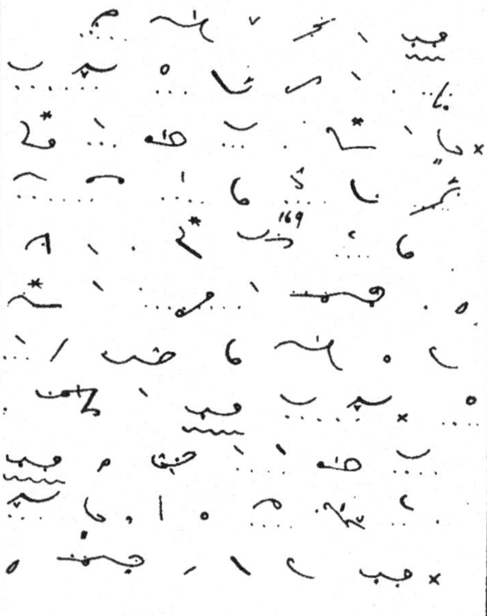

What to Do.

Prizes.

Exam. Fee.

A Course of Study.

To Teachers.

Make a *very* neat *copy* of the above passage, and send it to the Editor if possible on or before the 5th of December, 1893, so that the result may appear in the *January* number. The above paper may, however, be sent in for examination at *any later period* for the Certificate *only*.

Witness..

....

Competitor.

Private Students

Gold, Silver and Bronze Medals.

SPECIAL NOTICE.

Instead of sending 3d. every month, Competitors may compound by paying the Fee of 2/- for the complete set of Examinations. *(See pages 6 and 8).*

FOR DICTATION.

A SPEECH BY JOHN BRIGHT.

EVERY TEN WORDS INDICATED BY A SPACE.

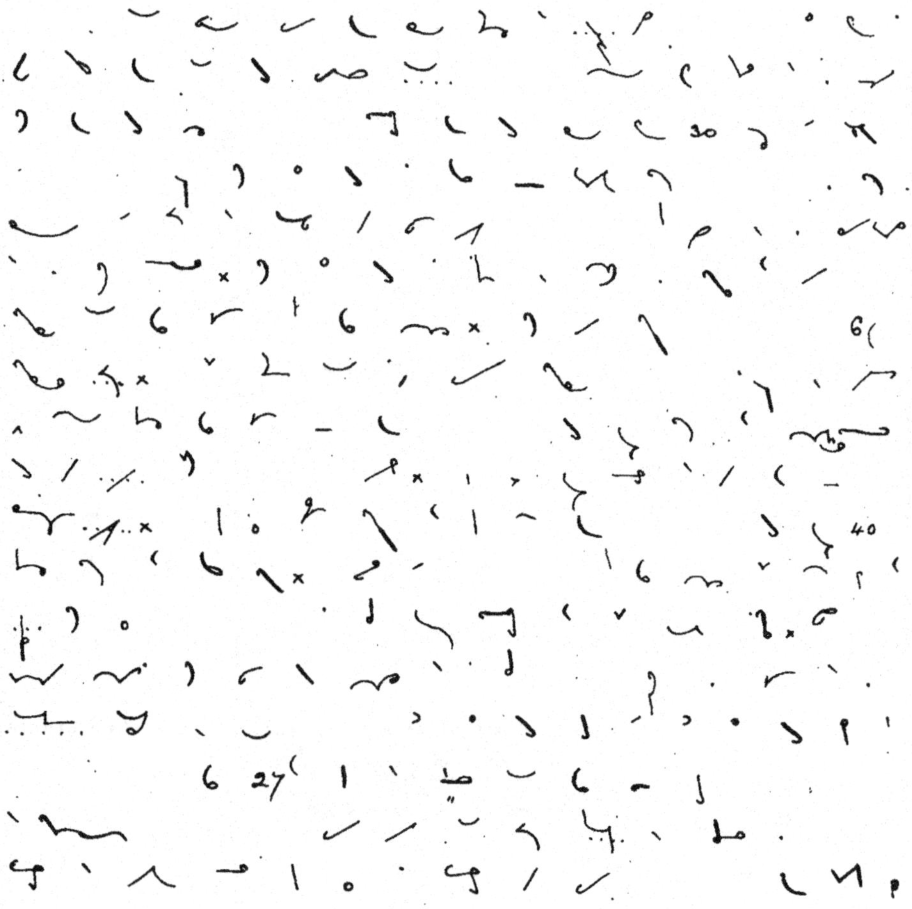

"THE YOUNG PHONOGRAPHER" EXAMINATIONS

FOR CERTIFICATES OF MERIT.

Dec., 1893.	Neatness.	June, 1894.	Advanced Vocalisation.
Jan., 1894.	Vocalisation.	July, "	Knowledge of Contractions.
Feb., "	Transcription.	Aug., "	Simple Phrasing.
Mar., "	Knowledge of Grammalogues.	Sept., "	Simple Exceptional Outlines.
April, "	Knowledge of Rule Numbers.	Oct., "	Business Phrases.
May, "	Knowledge of Advance Rules.	Nov. "	A Business Letter.

12 CERTIFICATES AND GRAND AWARD OF MERIT.

A Fee of 3d. is charged for each Examination (Grand Certificate free), or 2/-, if remitted on entering first Examination, is accepted in settlement of Examination Fees.

WHAT TEACHERS THINK OF "THE YOUNG PHONOGRAPHER."

PUBLISHED IN THE ORDER OF RECEIPT.

MR. DAVID LUMLEY.

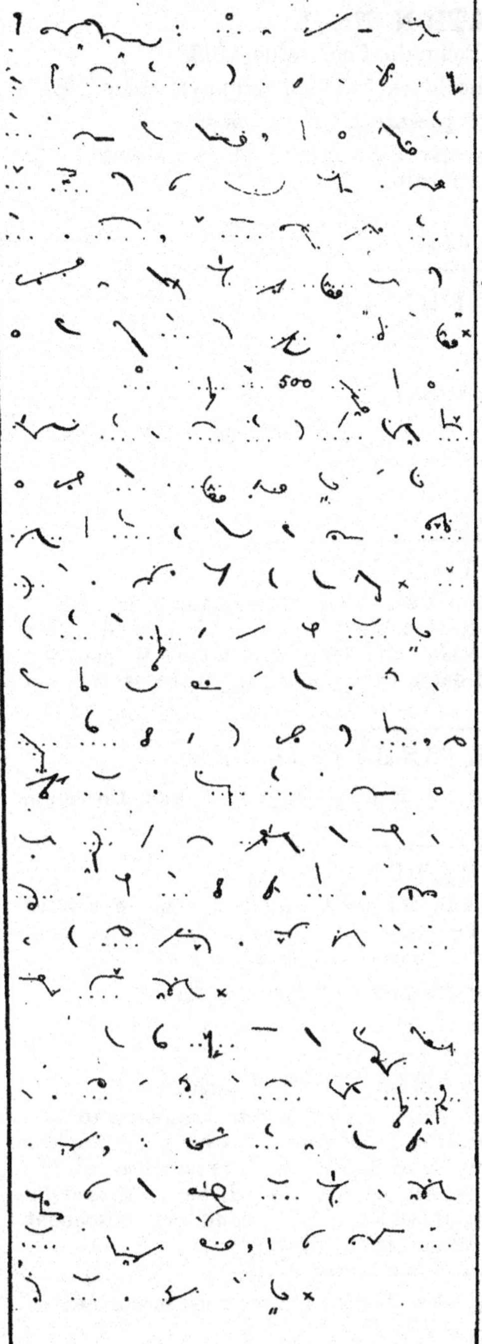

MR. A. MINTO NELSON.

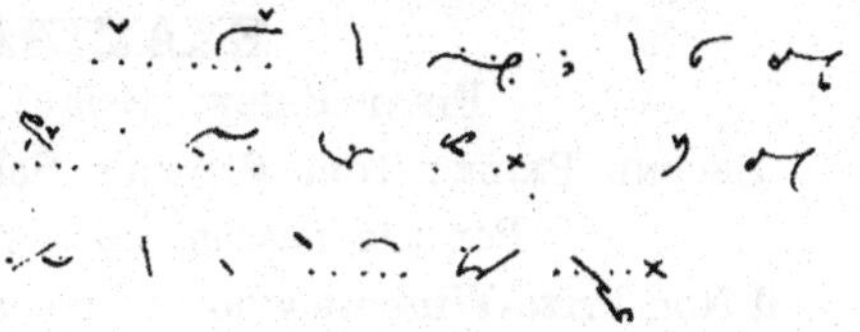

MR. C. T. BLANSHARD.

MR. C. W. TURNER, Bristol.

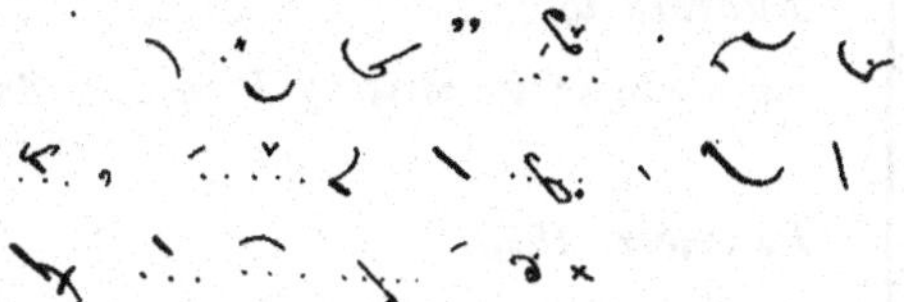

MR. D. BANKS, Warrington.

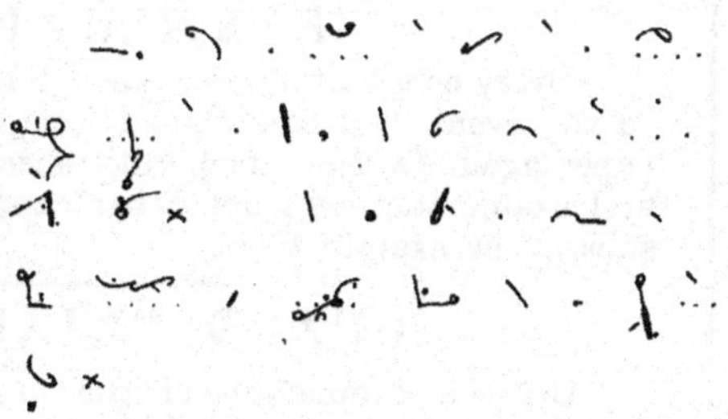

MR. H. ANDERTON, Sheffield.

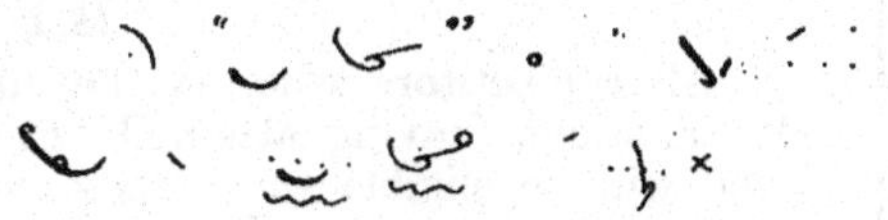

MR. H. TEES, Fulham.

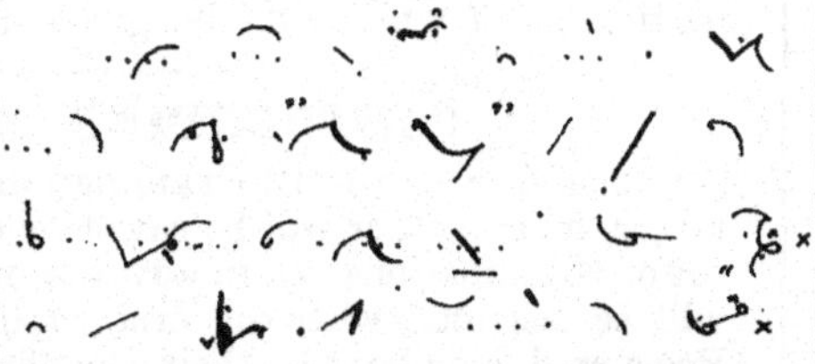

(To be continued).

GRAND COMPETITIONS FOR YOUNG PHONOGRAPHERS.

12 EXAMINATIONS FOR 12 CERTIFICATES.

SEE LIST ON PAGE 6.

EXAMINATION No. 1.

FIRST PRIZE: Swan Fountain Pen, value **10/6.**

SECOND PRIZE: Tom Brown's Schooldays (in Phonography), value **3/6.**

For the neatest copy of passage given on page 5.

All Non-Prize-Winners who receive 90 per cent. marks will be presented with the following Certificate of Merit:—

"THE YOUNG PHONOGRAPHER."

CERTIFICATE.

Awarded to ....

for neatness in writing Pitman's Shorthand.

OLIVER McEWAN, Editor.

December, 1893.

Registered No.

EXAMINATION FEE—3d.

Every competitor must send 3d. in stamps with the Examination Paper. In the event of a candidate failing, he or she will be allowed to send in the paper again (without fee) until successful, and temporary failure to pass the first examination will not debar candidates from competing in the second and subsequent examinations.

GRAND FINAL CERTIFICATE.

On the completion of the first 12 Examinations a Grand Complete Certificate will be awarded.

MEDALS!

All competitors who, at the end of the year, stand highest in the 12 Examinations (having attained not less than 1,100 marks out of a possible 1,200 will be eligible to compete in a special Examination for

1 Gold Medal, 1 Silver Medal, 1 Bronze Medal,

particulars of which will be given in the issue for December, 1894.

COMPOUNDING EXAMINATION FEES.

The Fees for the 12 Examinations will, if paid separately, amount to **3/-**; but, as much labour will be saved by *one fee* being paid to cover the complete set of Examinations, **2/-** in advance, in lieu of **3/-** in twelve remittances of 3d., will be accepted with the first paper. All competitors will be recognised by Registered Numbers of their Certificates, which in the second and subsequent Examinations must be *quoted* on the Examination Papers.

The Results of Examinations.—No. 1 will be announced in our next.

SEE GRAND COMPETITION (BACK PAGE), MEDALS, PRIZES AND CERTIFICATES.

THE

Young Phonographer,

— AND —

SHORTHAND BEGINNER'S MAGAZINE.

EDITED BY OLIVER McEWAN,

EDITOR "McEWAN'S PHONOGRAPHIC MAGAZINE," "THE SHORTHAND CRITIC AND REVIEW," AND "SHORTHAND NOTES AND QUERIES."

No. 3. VOL. I.] JANUARY, 1894. [Price 1d., 1/6 per annum, post free.

CONTENTS.

EDITORIAL CHAT.

OUR COMPETITIONS.

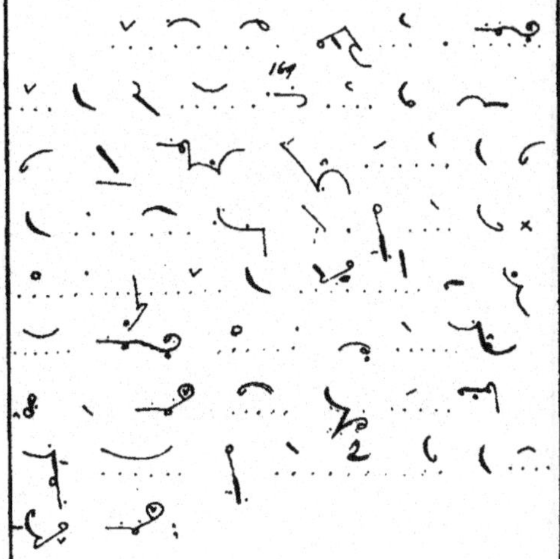

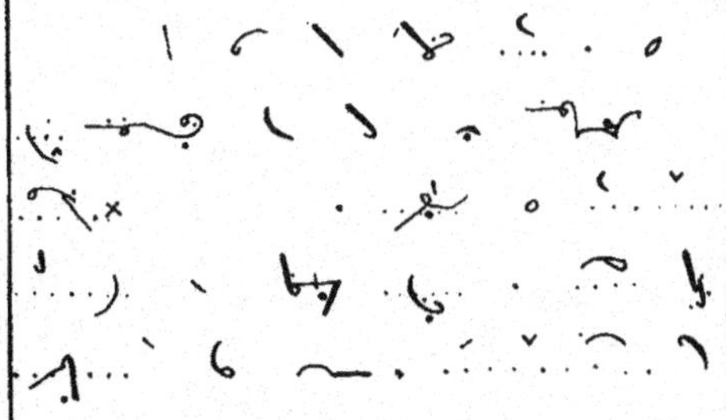

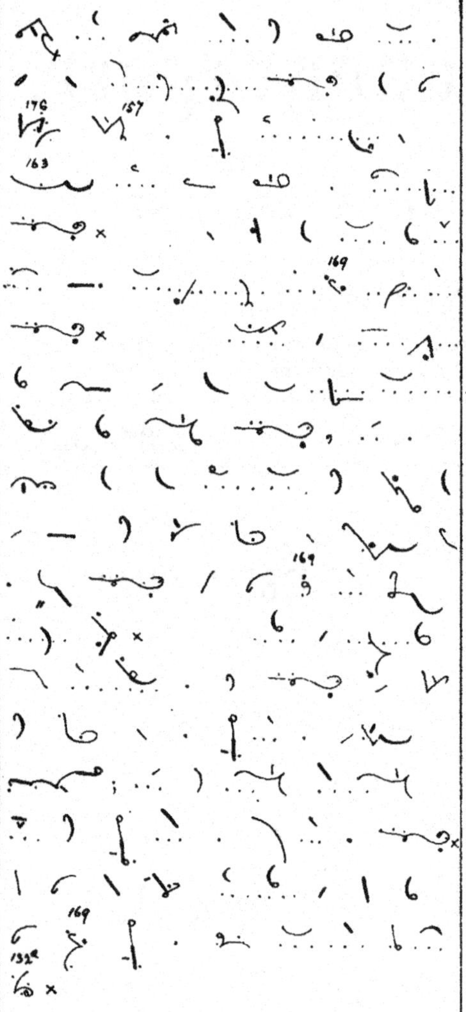

Bona Fide Learners only.

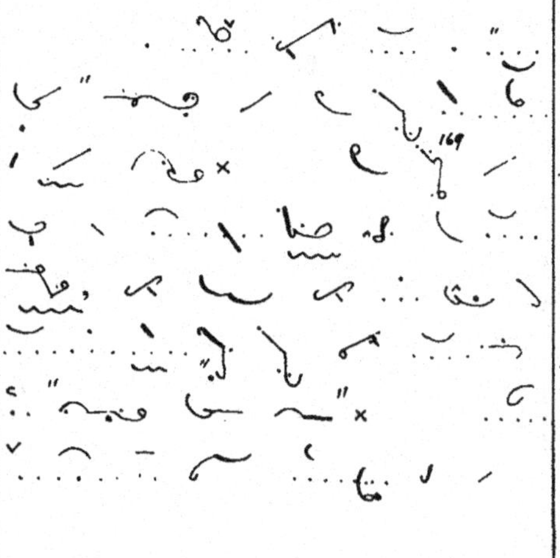

Oliver McEwan.

Some Beginners' Difficulties.

By C. P. Whittaker.

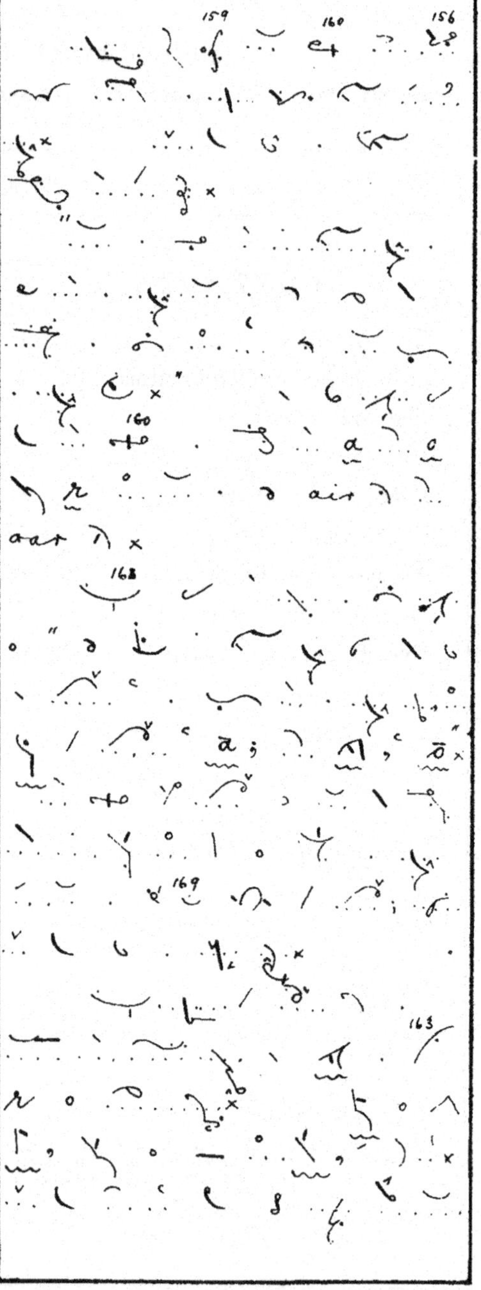

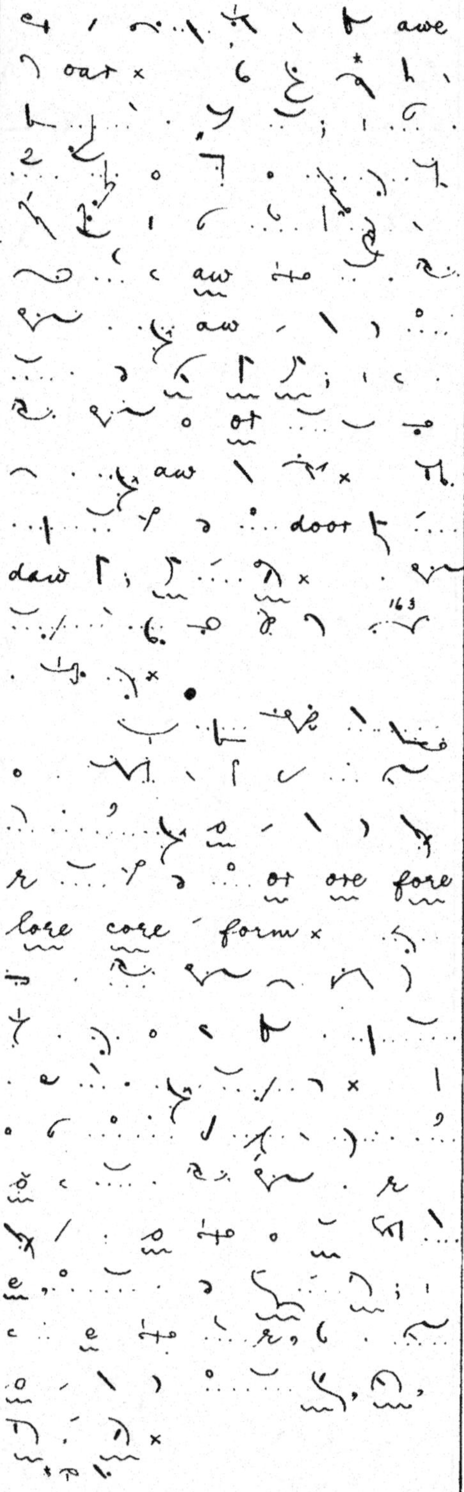

THE GRAMMALOGUES.

BY THE EDITOR.

(Continued).

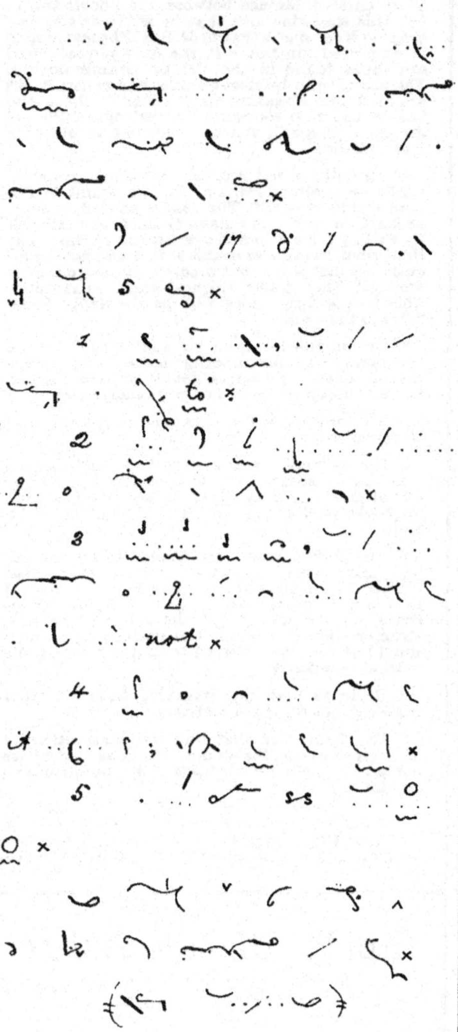

Shorthand Notes and Queries

IMPORTANT.

INSTRUCTIONS FOR READING THIS MAGAZINE.

THE chief difference between the Shorthand in this Magazine and that in *McEwan's Phonographic Magazine* is that in *M.P.M. Phraseography* is employed; in the *Y.P.* the only phrases used are those found in the list of Grammalogues. Yet, though the briefest outlines and contractions are used, this Magazine may be read by those who possess the *most elementary* knowledge of Phonography if they will strictly observe the following instructions:—

1. All outlines *not vocalised* are either *grammalogues* or *contractions*, and will be found in Pitman's "Instructor."* The reader should, as soon as possible, commit to memory the grammalogues by writing them over and over again. In the meantime, when the reader comes across an *unvocalised* outline which he cannot read, should search for it amongst the grammalogues and contractions. This frequent reference will be decidedly beneficial to the student.

2. Grammalogues may be distinguished from contractions by remembering that a grammalogue is represented by a *single*, *double* or *treble* letter, and a contraction by *two* or *more* such letters.

3. All words other than grammalogues and contractions are vocalised.

4. It is assumed that the reader is well acquainted with the consonants and vowels, and that he has also studied the Text Books so far as they include all *hooks*, *circles* and *loops*, and the halving principle.

5. All outlines which are formed in accordance with principles of abbreviation other than those noticed in the preceding paragraph, are indicated by the close proximity of figures. Those figures represent the number of the rule in the "Instructor" which explains the outline, and which should at once be referred to and studied if the outline is unknown.

6. Begin to read the Magazine from the *first* page—do not *dip* here and there.

7. By rigidly carrying out the instructions I have given above, the student will make advances in reading and in knowledge that will be surprising to him.

O. McE.

*"*The Grammalogues and Contractions*" *are separately published at 2d. by the Messrs. Pitman.*

HELPS TO THE STUDY.

BY THE EDITOR.

READING.

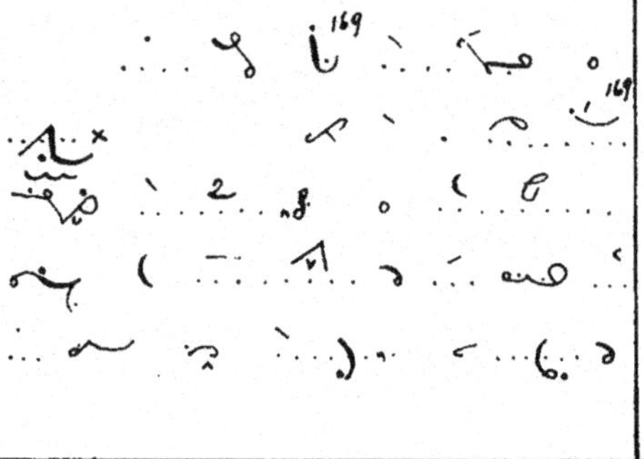

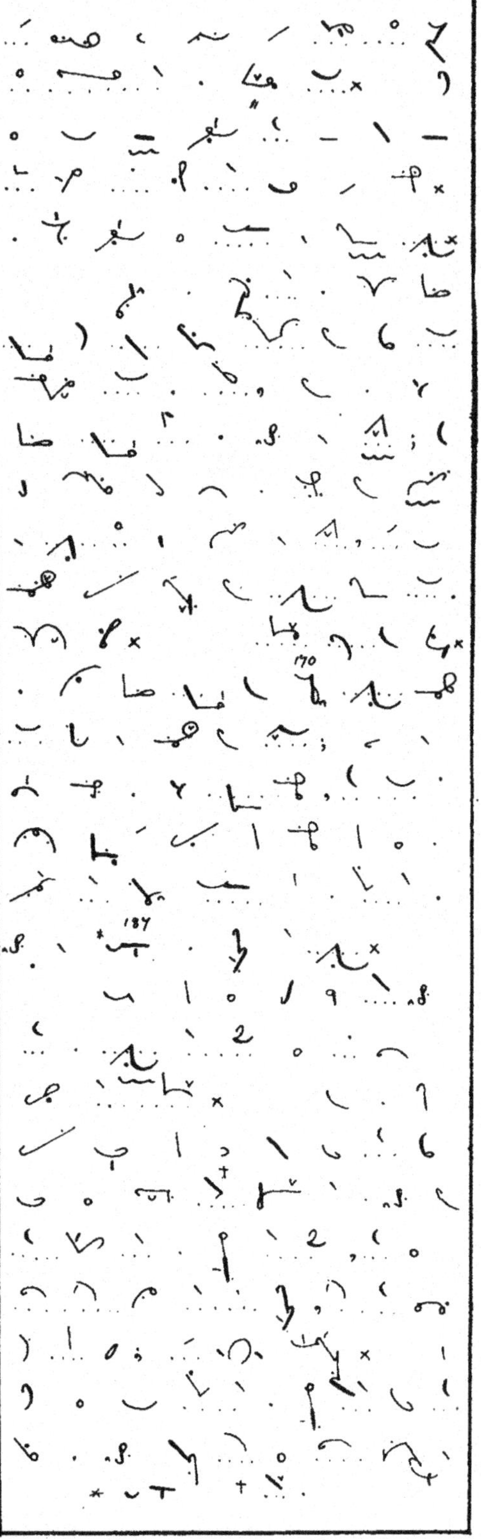

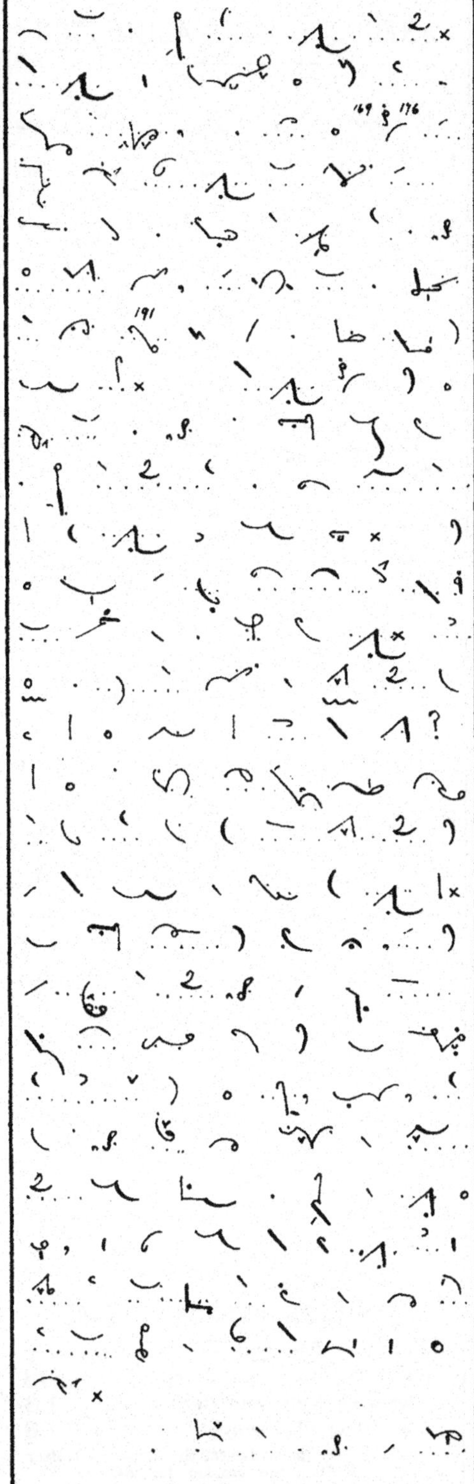

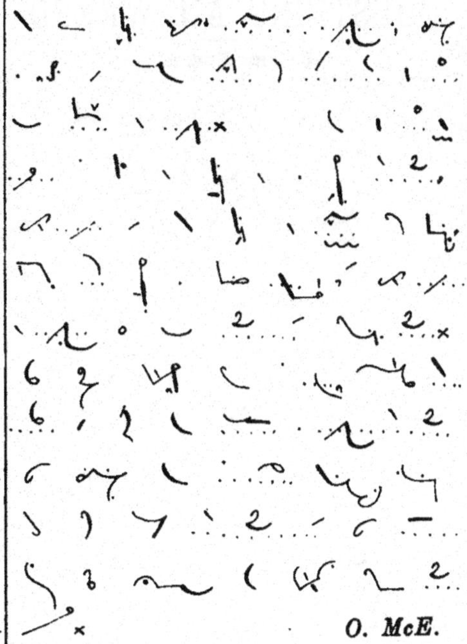

O. McE.

Exam. Paper No. 2.

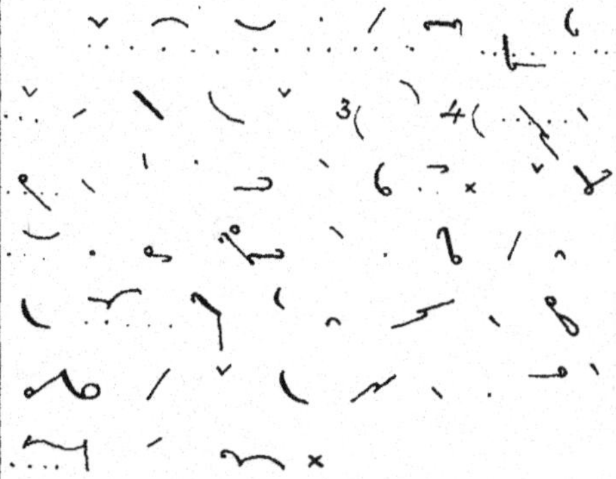

Make a *very* neat *copy* of the above passage, vocalising *all* outlines (whether grammalogues or not) except vowel logograms, such as *a should*, &c., and send it to the Editor if possible on or before the 7th of January, 1894, so that the result may appear in the *February* number. The above paper may, however, be sent in for examination at *any later period* for the Certificate *only*.

Papers must be witnessed. Read Conditions on page 8.

NOTE.—On this page grammalogues are vocalised, and in the last column *no* contractions are used.

QUESTIONS ANSWERED.

BY THE EDITOR.

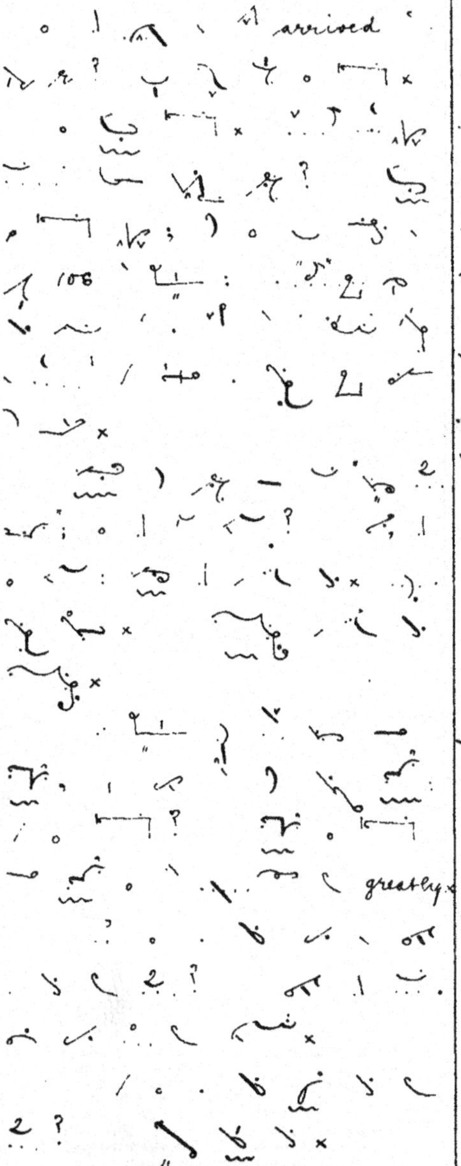

ANECDOTE OF WASHINGTON.

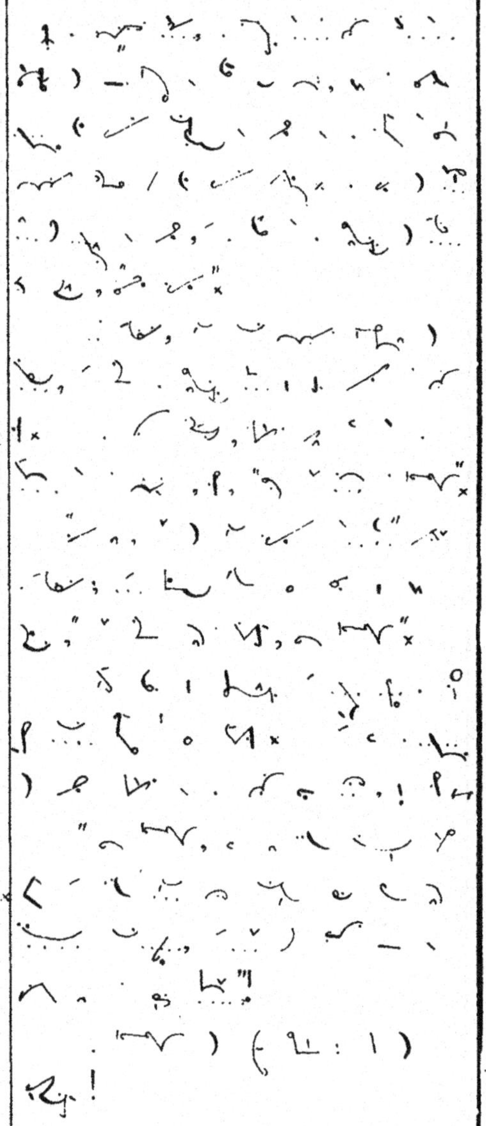

RESULT OF "THE YOUNG PHONOGRAPHER" COMPETITION No. 1.

FIRST PRIZE—Geo. Frederick Barling, 1, Poland Street, Oxford Street, W.

SECOND PRIZE—Thomas Hall, The Crofts, Nantwich, Cheshire.

Honors 100.—The Lady Mary Keppel, J. E. Ballard, A. I. Scott, F. Heckford, A. E. Hunt, W. Price, S. E. Lovatt, C. H. Spencer, A. O. Harper, W. Hills, A. E. Walker, S. Fuller, F. Chapman, W. J. Bettley, G. Stone, C. Dennis, T. Fletcher, J. Rauson, W. B. Duke, Ada R. Braham, A. Cole, E. C. Johnson, W. Lambe, H. Abbott, H. Sharpe, A. Brooks, E. R. Abbott, W. Banham, G. Pamely, Mary Ellen Pickard, R. Baggett, F. Roberts, M. F. Haworth, J. L. Flood, J. Gillespie, F. Gill, H. Costello, W. Willington, W. Bell, C. G. Cobb, G. B. Willsher, A. L. Spring, W. Milburn, W. McPherson, T. Moors, S. P. Auchinvole, J. W. Cooper, H. W. King, W. Horton, F. J. Gordge, W. H. Milward, J. McAlpin, W. J. Gear, E. Bettoney, E. R. Lee, S. Drinkwater, E. Hall, A. Robinson, H. Townend, G. L. G. Simmons, C. Watkins, J. Gilhespy, J. A. Stevenson, Harriet M. Young, A. W. Cox, C. S. Cowley, O. Carter, P. B. Hancock, W. J. Gill, W. Sanders, T. H. Lawson, J. P. Mason, H. Wiggins, J. J. Robinson, F. Shepherd, E. W. Wilson, H. Suetchford, W. Readd, Florence Nichols, E. A. Nichols, P. I. Dunn, J. E. Errington, A. Moss, P. L. Crew, G. H. Clarke, R. Snell, L. T. Cook, A. Burge, A. H. Pugson, J. M. Hannah, W. E. Agnew, S. Kirk, H. Sharpe, H. Rudkin, H. G. Lee, W. Shephard, T. Allsop, H. E. Hollingworth, H. Lee, T. R. Smithson S. R. Mills, G. Drinkwater, H. F. Gordon, G. Penlington.

98 Marks.—F. Plant, H. Smith.
97 „ E. J. Fowler, H. Elldred.
96 „ Evelyn Riley, H. Clayton.
95 „ W. A. B. Briggs, R. Evans.
90 „ H. Edwards, S. G. Skitteral.

"THE YOUNG PHONOGRAPHER" EXAMINATIONS

FOR CERTIFICATES OF MERIT.

Dec., 1893.	Neatness.*	June, 1894.	Advanced Vocalisation.
Jan., 1894.	Vocalisation.	July, „	Knowledge of Contractions.
Feb., „	Transcription.	Aug., „	Simple Phrasing.
Mar., „	Knowledge of Grammalogues.	Sept., „	Simple Exceptional Outlines.
April, „	Knowledge of Rule Numbers.	Oct., „	Business Phrases.
May, „	Knowledge of Advance Rules.	Nov. „	A Business Letter.

12 CERTIFICATES AND GRAND AWARD OF MERIT.

A Fee of 3d. is charged for each Examination (Grand Certificate free), or 2/-, if remitted on entering first Examination, is accepted in settlement of Examination Fees.

** Papers for this Exam. may still be sent in—Get No. 2.*

SEE NEXT PAGE.

GRAND COMPETITIONS FOR YOUNG PHONOGRAPHERS.

12 EXAMINATIONS FOR 12 CERTIFICATES.

SEE LIST ON PAGE 7.

EXAMINATION No. 2.

6/- FIRST PRIZE: Bound Volume *McEwan's Phonographic Magazine*, 1893.
4/- SECOND PRIZE: Bound Volume *McEwan's Shorthand Notes & Queries.*
2/6 THIRD PRIZE: Cloth-bound *Humours of Shorthand.*
1/6 FOURTH PRIZE: Paper Boards do.

For the neatest and most correctly vocalised copy of passage given on page 5.

All Non-Prize-Winners who receive 90 per cent. marks will be presented with the following Certificate of Merit:—

"THE YOUNG PHONOGRAPHER."

CERTIFICATE.

Awarded to ....

for thorough knowledge of elementary vowels used in Pitman's Shorthand.

OLIVER McEWAN, Editor.

January, 1894.

Registered No.

EXAMINATION FEE—3d.

Every competitor must send 3d. in stamps with the Examination Paper. In the event of a candidate failing, he or she will be allowed to send in the paper again (without fee) until successful, and temporary failure to pass the first examination will not debar candidates from competing in the second and subsequent examinations.

COMPOUNDING EXAMINATION FEES.

The Fees for the 12 Examinations will, if paid separately, amount to **3/-**; but, as much labour will be saved by *one fee* being paid to cover the complete set of Examinations, **2/-** in advance, in lieu of **3/-** in twelve remittances of 3d. will be accepted with the first paper. All competitors will be recognised by Registered Numbers of their Certificates, which in the second and subsequent Examinations must be *quoted* on the Examination Papers.

GRAND FINAL CERTIFICATE.

On the completion of the first 12 Examinations a Grand Complete Certificate will be awarded.

MEDALS!

All competitors who, at the end of the year, stand highest in the 12 Examinations (having attained not less than 1,100 marks out of a possible 1,200 will be eligible to compete in a special Examination for

1 Gold Medal, 1 Silver Medal, 1 Bronze Medal,

particulars of which will be given in the issue for December, 1894.

The Results of Examinations.—No. 2 will be announced in our next.

NOTE.—Every Paper must be Witnessed, the witness writing and signing the following declaration:—" Written in my presence, without assistance or reference to books."

SEE GRAND COMPETITION (BACK PAGE), MEDALS, PRIZES AND CERTIFICATES.

THE

Young Phonographer,

— AND —

SHORTHAND BEGINNER'S MAGAZINE.

EDITED BY OLIVER McEWAN,

EDITOR "McEWAN'S PHONOGRAPHIC MAGAZINE," "THE SHORTHAND CRITIC AND REVIEW," AND "SHORTHAND NOTES AND QUERIES."

No. 4. VOL. I.] FEBRUARY, 1894. [Price 1d., 1/6 per annum, post free.

CONTENTS.

A STORY.

TOM'S ADVENTURE.

BY OLIVER McEWAN.

(*Chiefly in Monosyllables*).

CHAPTER I.—ON THE REEF.

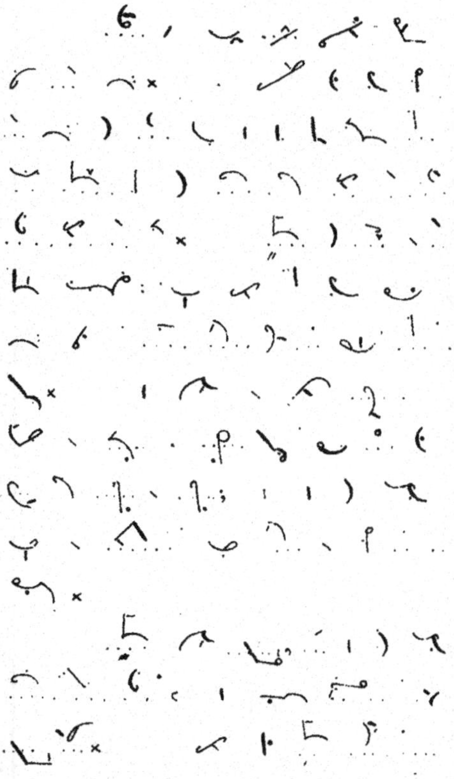

Published by JOHN HEYWOOD, London & Manchester.

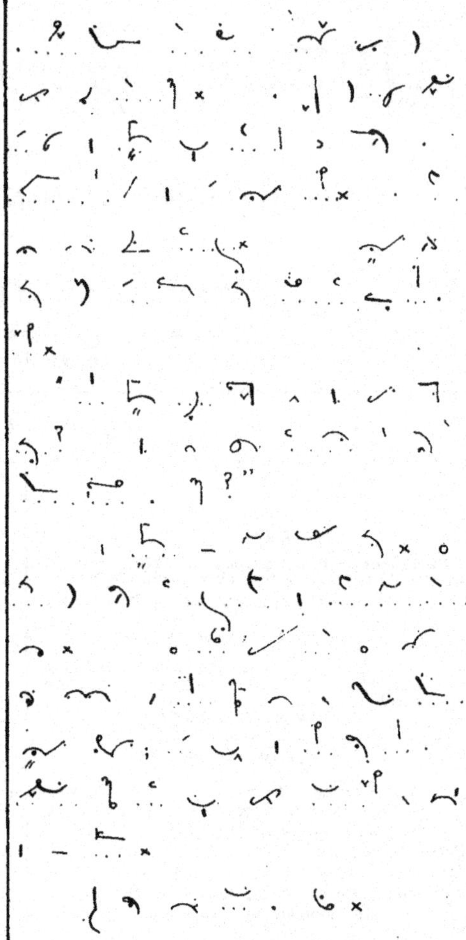

(To be concluded next month).

SOME MNEMONIC AIDS

TO THE STUDY OF PHONOGRAPHY.

PARTLY ORIGINAL, PARTLY FROM THE TEXT BOOKS.

By C. T. Blanshard, M.A., F.N.P.S., of the Oxford School of Shorthand.

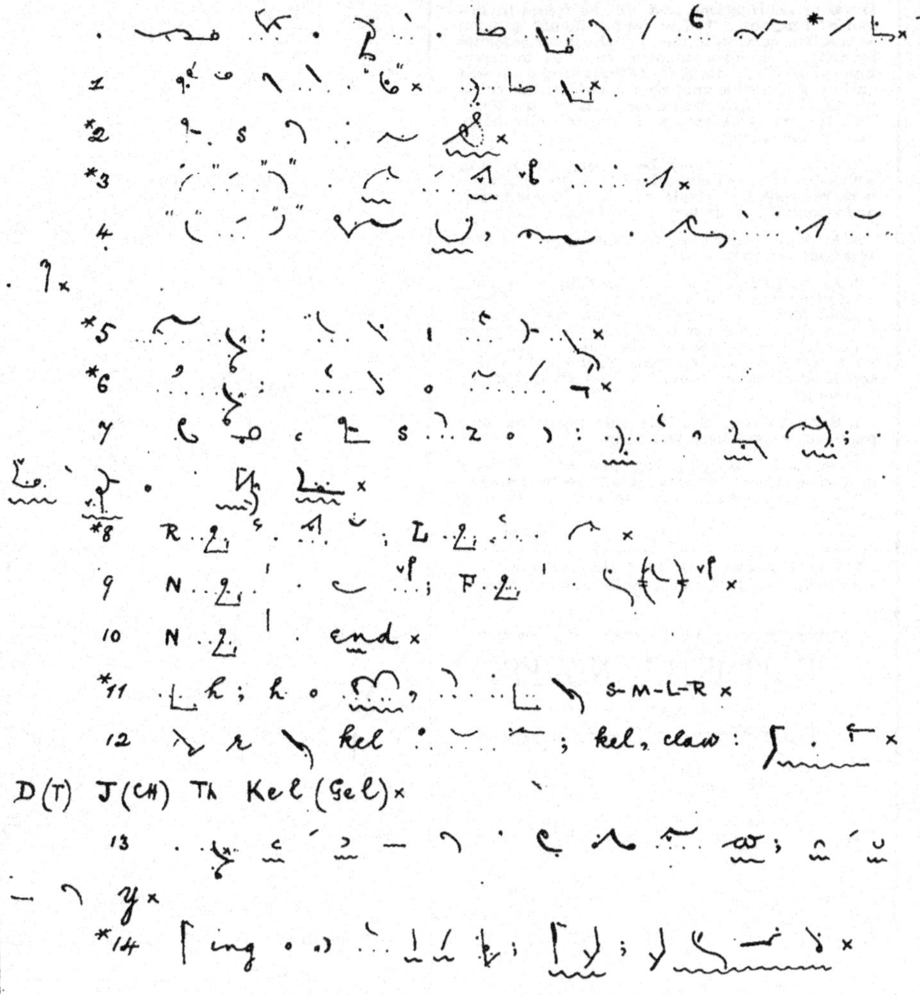

THE EDITOR'S WORKS.

IMPORTANT.

INSTRUCTIONS FOR READING THIS MAGAZINE.

This Magazine is written in three grades of Phonography.

1. All outlines *not vocalised* are either *grammalogues* or *contractions*, and will be found in Pitman's "Instructor."* The reader should, as soon as possible, commit to memory the grammalogues by writing them over and over again. In the meantime, when the reader comes across an *unvocalised* outline which he cannot read, should search for it amongst the grammalogues and contractions. This frequent reference will be decidedly beneficial to the student.

2. Grammalogues may be distinguished from contractions by remembering that a grammalogue is represented by a *single, double* or *treble* letter, and a contraction by *two* or *more* such letters.

3. All words other than grammalogues and contractions are vocalised.

4. All outlines which are formed in accordance with principles of abbreviation other than those noticed in the preceding paragraph, are indicated by the close proximity of figures. Those figures represent the number of the rule in the "Instructor" which explains the outline, and which should at once be referred to and studied if the outline is unknown.

5. Begin to read the Magazine from the *first* page—do not *dip* here and there.

6. By rigidly carrying out the instructions I have given above, the student will make advances in reading and in knowledge that will be surprising to him.

O. McE.

*"*The Grammalogues and Contractions*" *are separately published at 2d. by the Messrs. Pitman.*

EDITORIAL NOTES.

Last Month's Competition.

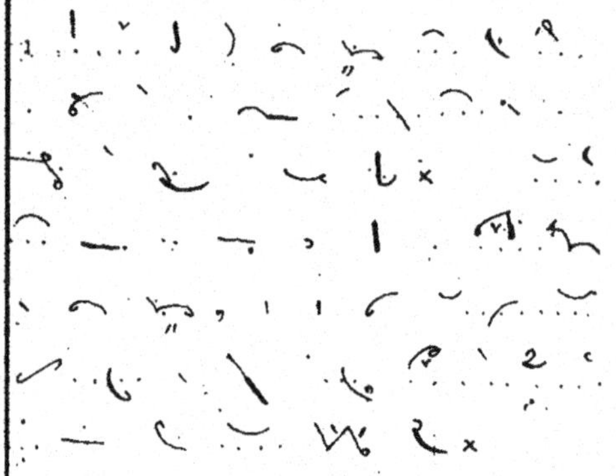

Still Open.

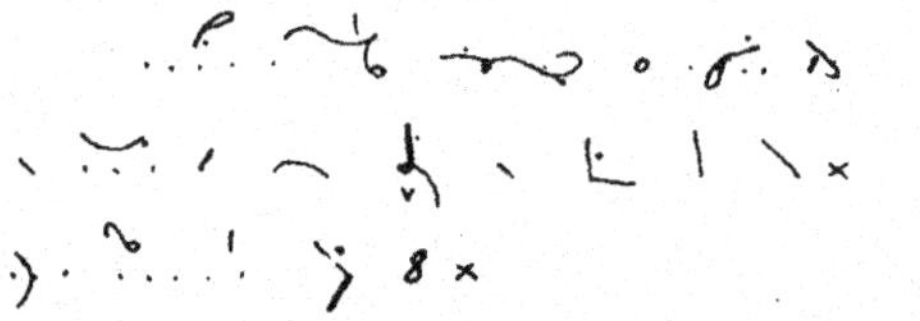

Easy Readings.

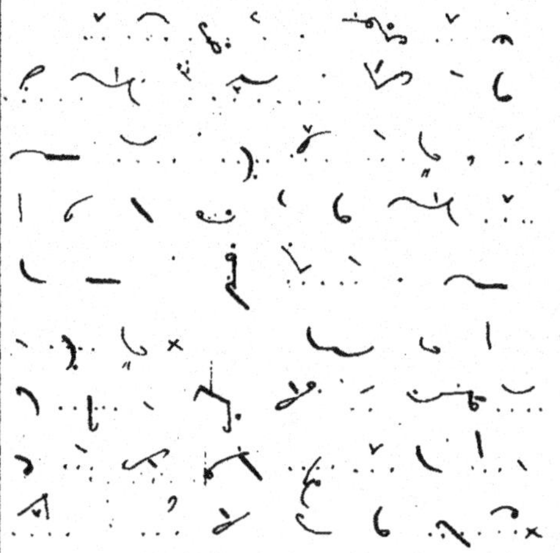

NEXT MONTH!

"Schooldays of Sherlock Holmes."

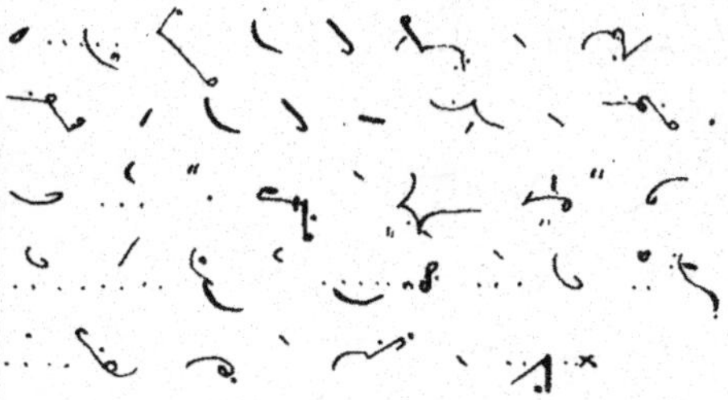

Oliver McEwan.

QUESTIONS ANSWERED.

BY THE EDITOR.

STUDY.

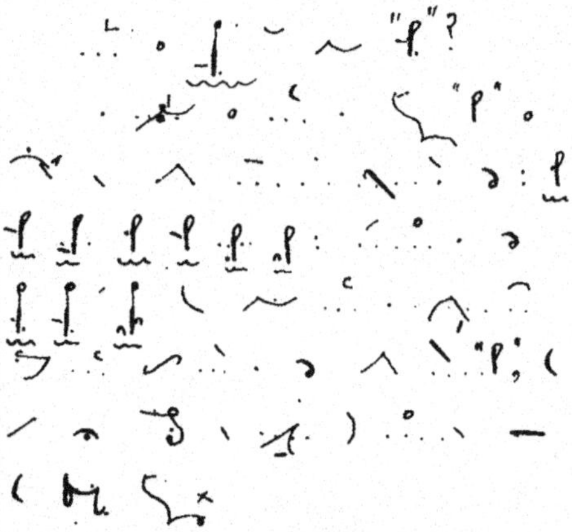

POSITION.

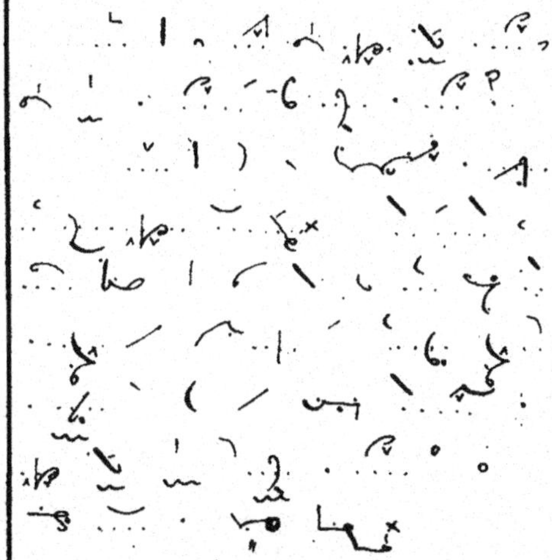

DOUBTLESS.

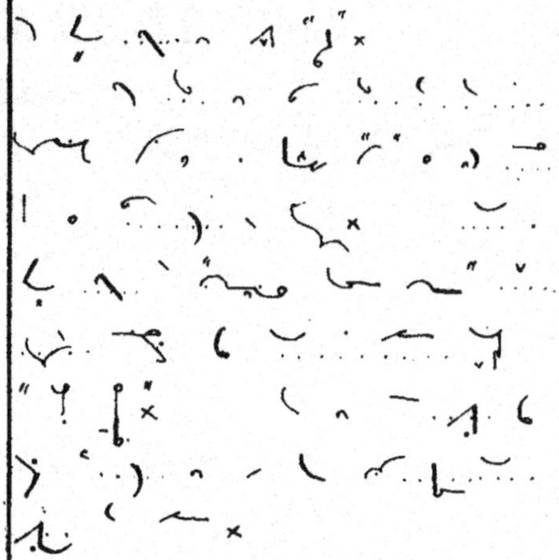

RIGHT

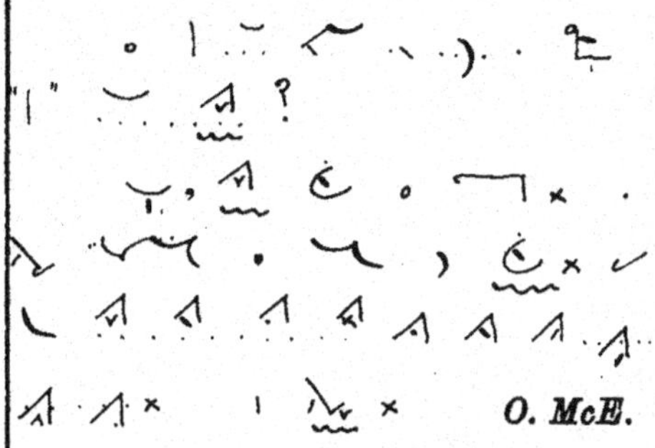

O. McE.

EXAMINATION No. 3.

PAPER.

Transcribe neatly the paragraph in preceding column under the heading "Position," and send to the Editor. See Conditions on page 8.

EASY REPORTING STYLE.—VOCALISED.

THE GRAMMALOGUES.

(Concluded.)

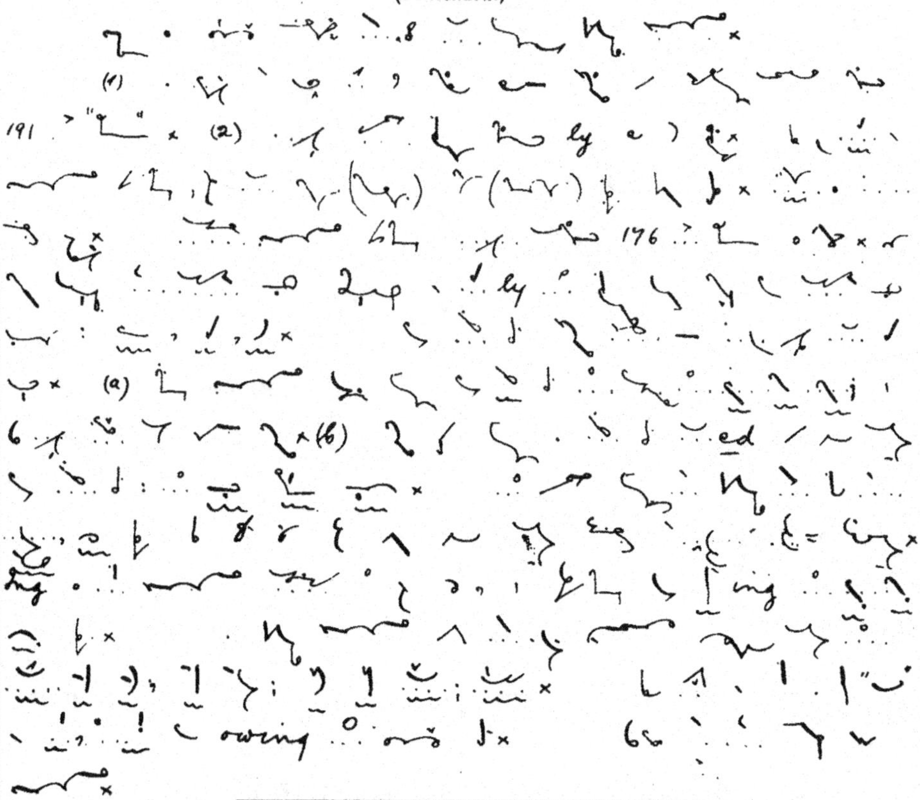

JOHN'S CAKE AND HIS NEW SIXPENCE.

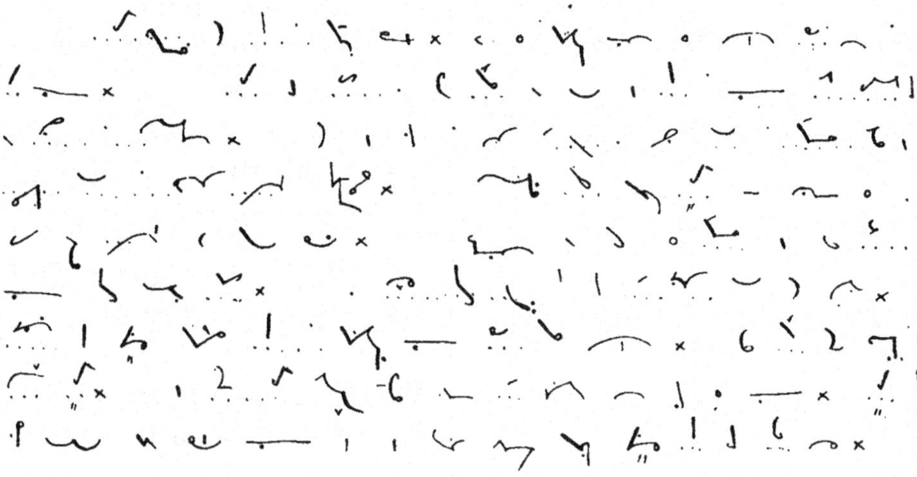

(To be continued.)

RESULT OF "THE YOUNG PHONOGRAPHER" COMPETITION No. 2.

FIRST PRIZE—The Lady Mary Keppel, 65, Princes Gate, S.W.
SECOND PRIZE—James F. Herdman, 15, Hannah Street, Newcastle.
THIRD PRIZE—John C. Cole, 28, Silver Street, Whitby.
FOURTH PRIZE—John Leitch, 12, Maryhall Street, Kirkcaldy.

Honours 100.—A. L. Spring, J. McAlpin, T W. Hall, P. B. Hancock, J. J. Robinson, G. F. Barling, E. J. Towler, G. L. G. Simmons, W. J. Gear, C. Delabene Marsden, W. B. Duke, E. Howse, A. Moss, G. Drinkwater, A. H. Pugson, F. Nichols, H. Sharpe.

99 Marks.—A. Freeman, T. B. Wisdom, E. R. Lee, F. Shepherd, F. Heckford, C. H. Watkins, R. H. Ingram, S. E. Lovatt, R. F. Baggett, J. Gascoigne, A. E. Hunt, J. Grieves, E. Johnson, R. Taylor, E. J. Mansfield, W. McPherson, O. Carter, M. Cowell, E. C. Johnson, W. J. Gill, W. Banham, G. Pamely, A. Brooks, H. Rudkin, E. Abbott, H. Abbott, J. Pritchard.

98 Marks.—S. Drinkwater, P. Child, T. B. Webster, P. A. Holroyd, S. Kirk, H. Sharpe, T. R. Murray, M. E. Pickard, A. E. Weech, J. Speight, E. Nichols.

97 Marks.—T. H. Lawson.

95 „ T. Fletcher.

90 Marks.—H. Rogers, J. W. Cooper.

"THE YOUNG PHONOGRAPHER" EXAMINATIONS
FOR CERTIFICATES OF MERIT.

Dec., 1893,	Neatness.*	June, 1894.	Advanced Vocalisation.
Jan., 1894.	Vocalisation.*	July, „	Knowledge of Contractions.
Feb., „	Transcription.	Aug., „	Simple Phrasing.
Mar., „	Knowledge of Grammalogues.	Sept., „	Simple Exceptional Outlines.
April, „	Knowledge of Rule Numbers.	Oct., „	Business Phrases.
May, „	Knowledge of Advance Rules.	Nov. „	A Business Letter.

12 CERTIFICATES AND GRAND AWARD OF MERIT.

A Fee of 3d. is charged for each Examination (Grand Certificate free), or 2/-, if remitted on entering first Examination, is accepted in settlement of Examination Fees.

* *Papers for this Exam. may still be sent in—Get No. 2.*

SEE NEXT PAGE.

GRAND COMPETITIONS FOR YOUNG PHONOGRAPHERS.

12 EXAMINATIONS FOR 12 CERTIFICATES.

SEE LIST ON PAGE 7.

EXAMINATION No. 3.

6/- First Prize: Bound Volume *McEwan's Phonographic Magazine*, 1893.
4/- Second Prize: Bound Volume *McEwan's Shorthand Notes & Queries.*
2/6 Third Prize: Cloth-bound *Humours of Shorthand.*
1/6 Fourth Prize: Paper Boards do.

For the neatest and most correct transcription of passage given on page 5.

All Non-Prize-Winners who receive 90 per cent. marks will be presented with the following Certificate of Merit:—

"THE YOUNG PHONOGRAPHER."

CERTIFICATE.

Awarded to ....

for correcting transcription of Shorthand into Longhand.

OLIVER McEWAN, Editor.

February, 1894.

Registered No.

EXAMINATION FEE—3d. *each* Examination.

Every competitor must send 3d. in stamps with the Examination Paper. In the event of a candidate failing, he or she will be allowed to send in the paper again (without fee) until successful, and temporary failure to pass the first examination will not debar candidates from competing in the second and subsequent examinations.

GRAND FINAL CERTIFICATE.

On the completion of the first 12 Examinations a Grand Complete Certificate will be awarded.

MEDALS!

All competitors who, at the end of the year, stand highest in the 12 Examinations (having attained not less than 1,100 marks out of a possible 1,200 will be eligible to compete in a special Examination for

1 Gold Medal, 1 Silver Medal, 1 Bronze Medal,

particulars of which will be given in the issue for December, 1894.

The Results of Examinations.—No. 2 will be announced in our next.

NOTE.—Every Paper must be Witnessed, the witness writing and signing the following declaration:—"Written in my presence, without assistance or reference to books.

"Not Known" at Pitman's. Sole Publisher, JOHN HEYWOOD, 2, Amen Corner, London; and Deansgate, Manchester.

THE

Young Phonographer,

— AND —

SHORTHAND BEGINNER'S MAGAZINE.

EDITED BY OLIVER McEWAN,

EDITOR "McEWAN'S PHONOGRAPHIC MAGAZINE," "THE SHORTHAND CRITIC AND REVIEW,' AND "SHORTHAND NOTES AND QUERIES."

No. 5. VOL. I.] MARCH, 1894. [Price 1d., 1/6 per annum, post free.

CONTENTS.

IMPORTANT.

INSTRUCTIONS FOR READING THIS MAGAZINE.

This Magazine is written in three grades of the Learner's Style of Phonography.

All outlines *not vocalised* are *grammalogues*, and will be found in Pitman's "First" Primer.

In the first story many grammalogues are vocalised, so as to enable the most elementary students to read it.

Begin to read the Magazine from the *first* page—do not *dip* here and there.

THE

SCHOOLDAYS OF SHERLOCK

WITH HIS FRIENDS,

TOM, DICK, AND HARRY.

INTRODUCTION.

WHEN

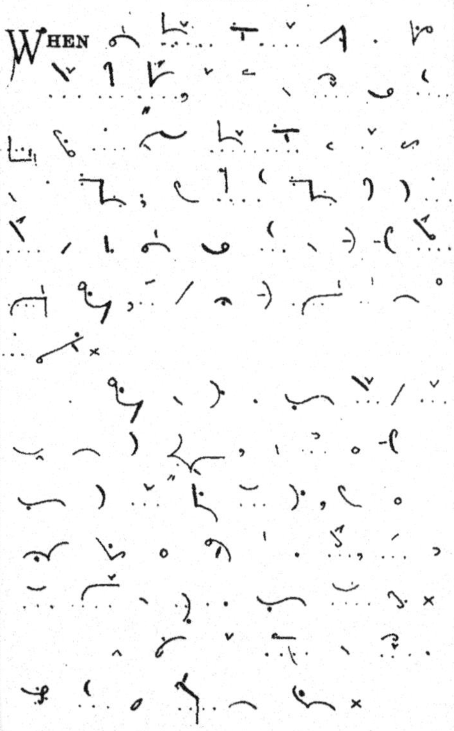

Published by JOHN HEYWOOD, London & Manchester.

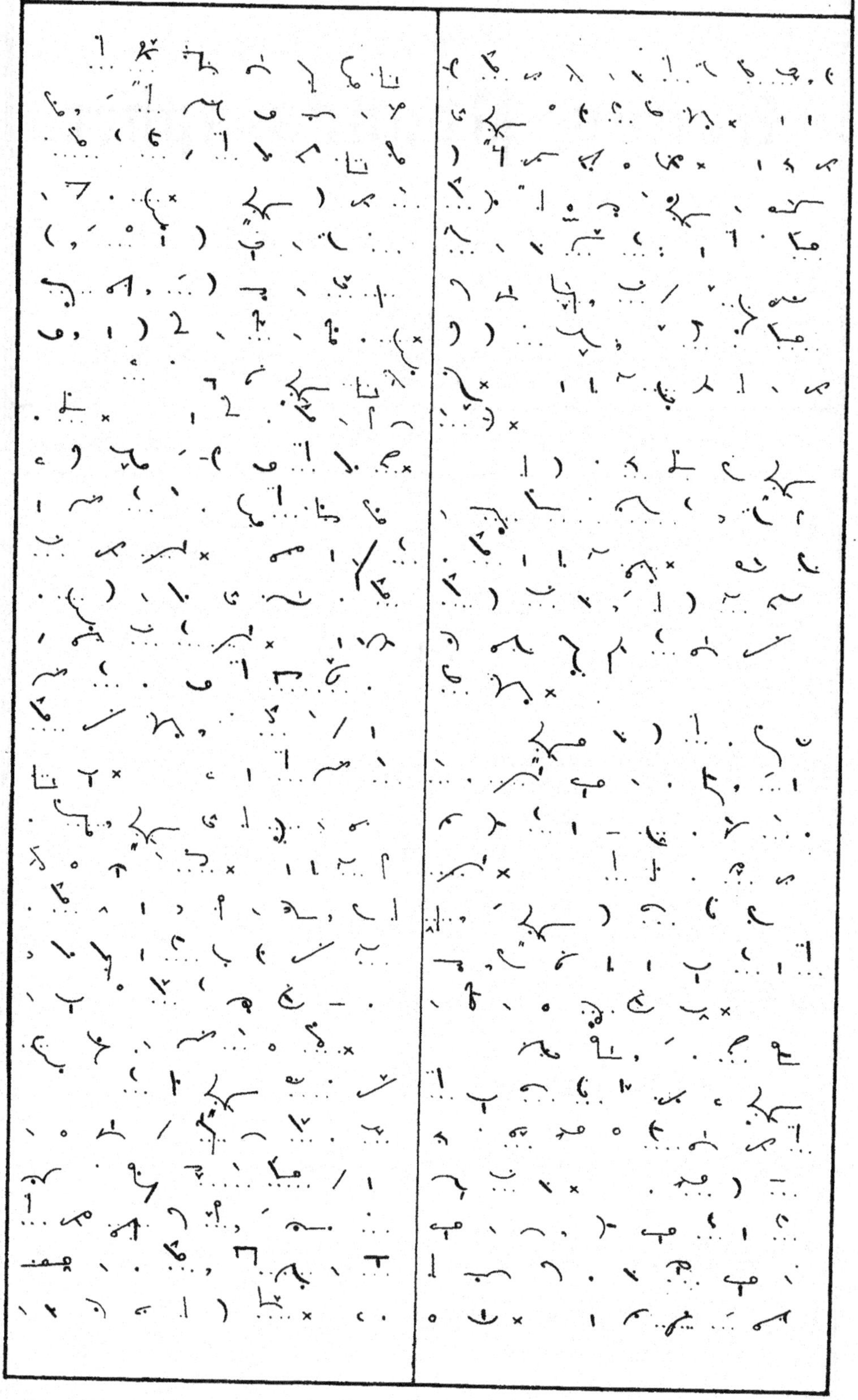

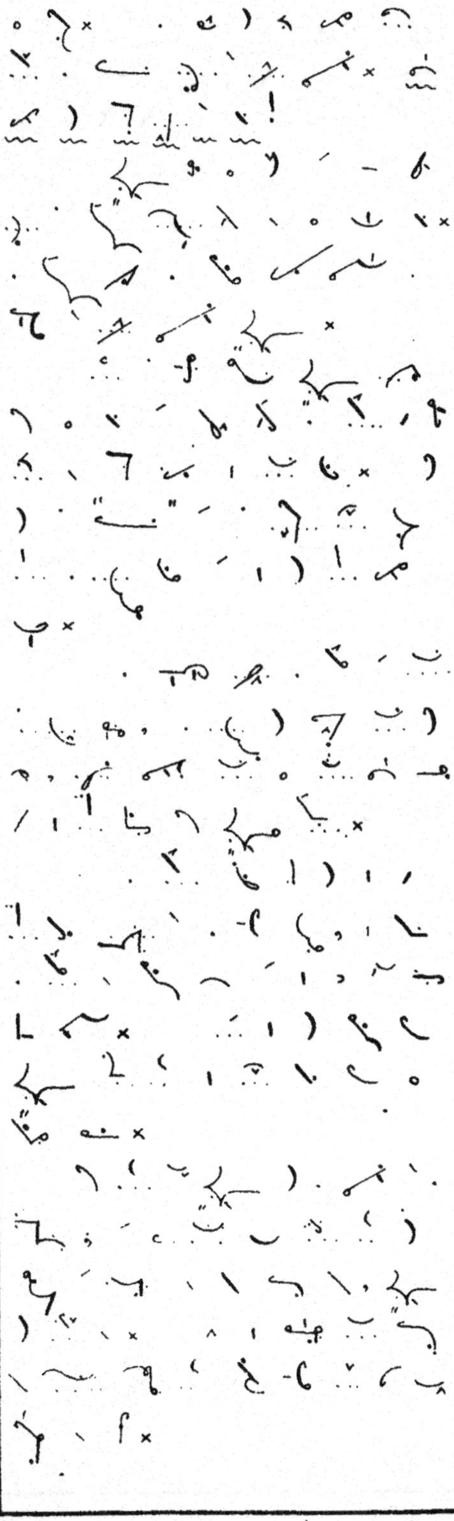

JOHN'S CAKE—*continued.*

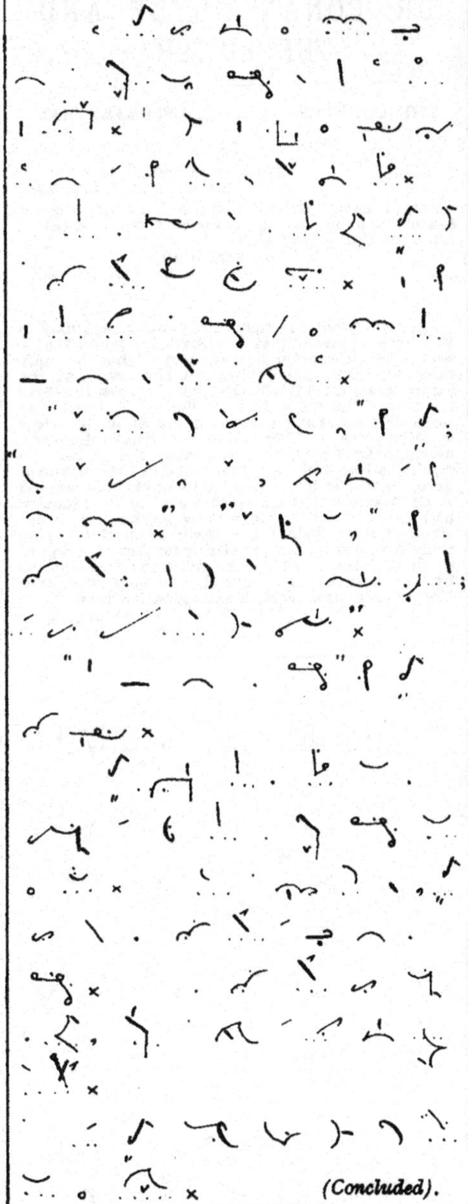

(Concluded).

DR. CONAN DOYLE AND THE EDITOR.

THE COURTESY (?) OF A LITERARY MAN.

KINHAUS HOTEL,
DAVOS PLATZ, *Feb. 2, 1894.*

SIR,—I have instructed my solicitor to proceed against you on the appearance of your so-called Sherlock Holmes stories.

Yours faithfully,
A. CONAN DOYLE.

I have altered the title of the story beginning in this issue. I regret that Dr. Doyle imagined that I would trespass upon any literary rights he may possess in the name "Sherlock Holmes." At the same time, I am advised that had I chosen to retain the title, "The Schooldays of Sherlock Holmes," the law could not have prevented my doing so. Nor would my use of "Sherlock Holmes" have done any harm to Dr. Doyle, for at the very time when the public had become most interested in that mythical hero, he was killed with a suddenness that caused some to assert that the author's vivid imagination had run to "seed." It will be interesting to see whether this incident has again aroused it; if so there may yet appear something further with regard to the "deceased Sherlock," when the title created by me may come in useful, and save the good Doctor again overtaxing his imaginative powers.

O. McEWAN.

THE EDITOR'S CHAT.

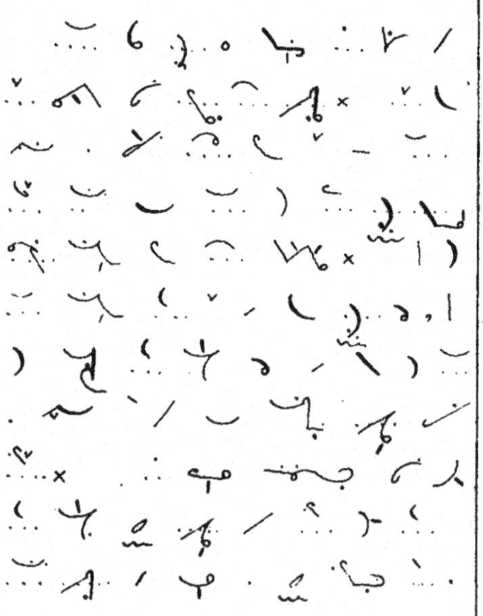

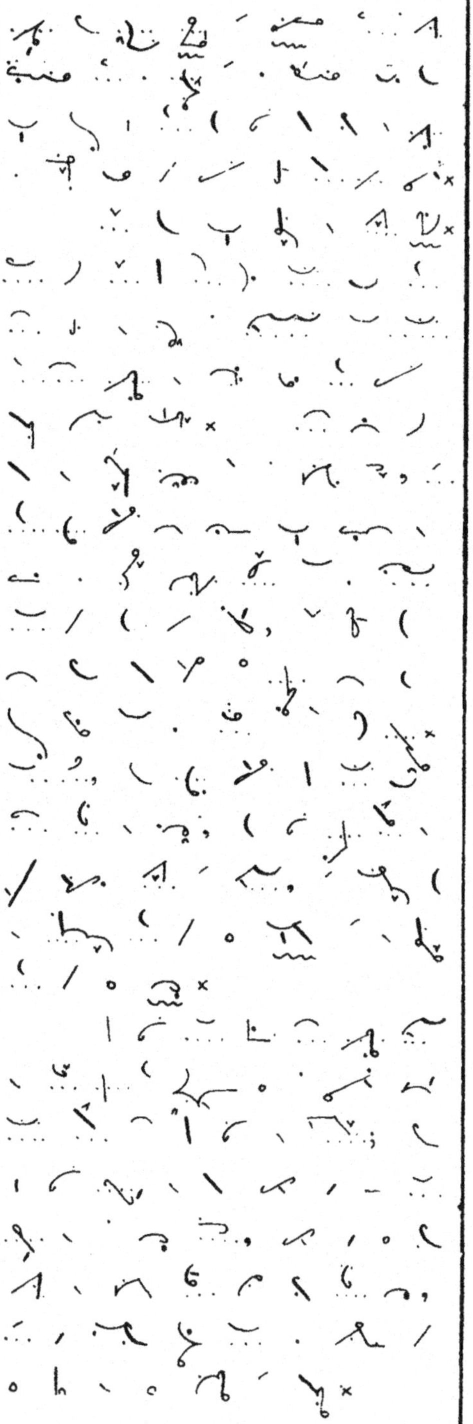

Successful Boys.

New Heroes.

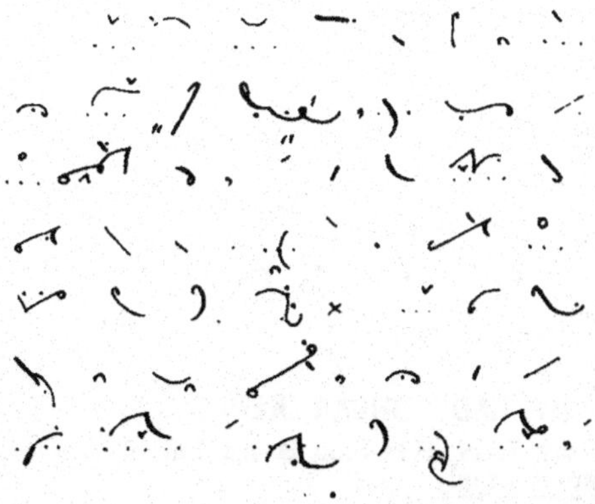

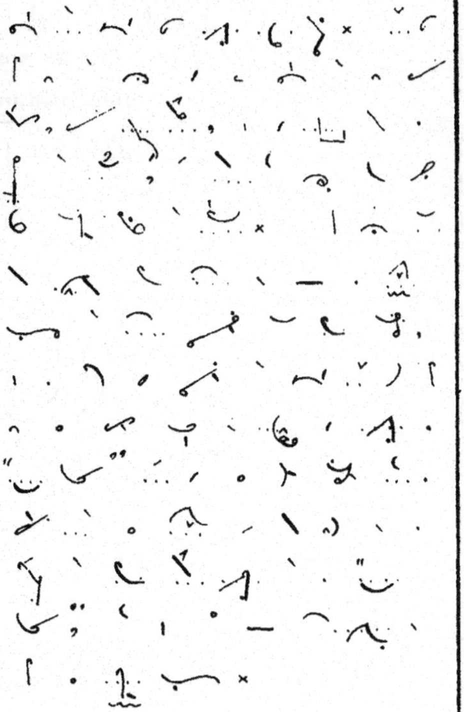

Don't Go to Pitman's for "The Young Phonographer."

Mr. J. Heywood's (next door),
2, Amen Corner, E.C.

O. McEwan.

TOM'S ADVENTURE.

BY THE EDITOR.

(Continued from last Month).

CHAPTER II.—MISSING.

(To be continued).

RESULT OF
"THE YOUNG PHONOGRAPHER" COMPETITION No. 3.

FIRST. PRIZE.—G. DRINKWATER, 3, St. Philips Road, Dalston, N.E.
SECOND PRIZE.—A. O. HARPUR, The Mansion, Old Whittington, Chesterfield.
THIRD PRIZE.—G. L. A. LEWIS, 6, Dawson Street, Dublin.
FOURTH PRIZE.—J. C. COSSAR, 205, Georgie Road, Edinburgh.

Erratum:—For James Herdman, in Feb. issue, read JOHN GILHESPY, 42, Camborne Grove, Gateshead, winner of the Second Prize.

HONOURS, 100.—The Lady Mary Keppel, H. Rudkin, C. H. Watkins, W. H. Stanley, E. Howse, E. Moors, A. H. Pugsom, O. Carter, T. R. Murray, L. T. Cook, E. J. Fowler, W. Willington, J. E. Ballard, J. R. Foster, J. Gilhespy, T. W. Corker, H. Parfitt, C. W. Hill, H. Shawcroft, W. J. Gill, E. J. Tansley, Mary Jane Brown, W. A. B. Briggs, Mary Ellen Pickard, D. Livesey, H. Parker, F. W. Hooper, C. H. Brown, A. G. Ring, J. W. Oldfield, G. L. G. Simmons, W. G. Martin, W. Fuller, W. Woodburne, H. Edwards, R. Taylor, W. Edwards, W. J. Gear, E. Haines, J. S. Monk, M. MacLeod, L. F. Warner, J. H. Pym, W. Grassick, W. B. Duke, E. Trickett, R. Campbell, A. Burge, J. C. Cole, J. T. Oldfield, M. H. Jackson, T. W. Hall, S. P. Auchinvole, L. Franklin, L. Cook, J. J. Robinson, W. Maynard, S. E. Lovatt, P. Child, E. C. Johnson, W. Watson, M. Cowell, Nelly Donald, T. Moors. E. F. Edsall, J. Carriss, T. Heywood, Annie M. Smith, Stanley Drinkwater, W. M. Young, J. J. Woodman, H. Preston, G. Stone, C. Walker, T. J. M. Marshall, H. Edwards, J. W. Cooper, A. E. Weech, G. H. Morris, Frances J. Barker, E. Richards, F. J. P. Buckland, S. Kirk, A. W. Cox, F. Heckford, A. E. Knight, P. B. Hancock, S. T. Ashford, A. L. Spring, G. F. Barling, E. Hawkins, J. Royce, W. E. Agnew, E. J. Mansfield, H. F. Gordon, A. Freeman, L. Kate Porter, H. W. Lee, W. McPherson, M. P. Baldeson, Violet Smallhorn, H. W. Turner, R. H. Ingram, J. Leitch, F. J. Gordge, L. Stubbs, C. H. Gibson.

95 MARKS.—G. Porritt, F. Gill, A. Moss, J. Watson, R. F. Baggett.

NOTE.—The above includes all Papers received up to February 8th.

"THE YOUNG PHONOGRAPHER" EXAMINATIONS
FOR CERTIFICATES OF MERIT.

Dec., 1893.	Neatness.*	June, 1894.	Advanced Vocalisation.
Jan., 1894.	Vocalisation.*	July, "	Knowledge of Contractions.
Feb., "	Transcription.*	Aug., "	Simple Phrasing.
Mar., "	Knowledge of Grammalogues.	Sept., "	Simple Exceptional Outlines.
April, "	Knowledge of Rule Numbers.	Oct., "	Business Phrases.
May, "	Knowledge of Advance Rules.	Nov. "	A Business Letter.

12 CERTIFICATES AND GRAND AWARD OF MERIT.

A Fee of 3d. is charged for each Examination (Grand Certificate free), or 2/-, if remitted on entering first Examination, is accepted in settlement of Examination Fees.

** Papers for this Exams. may still be sent in—Get Back Numbers.*

GRAND COMPETITIONS FOR YOUNG PHONOGRAPHERS.

12 EXAMINATIONS FOR 12 CERTIFICATES.

SEE LIST ON PAGE 7.

EXAMINATION No. 3.

6/- First Prize: Bound Volume *McEwan's Phonographic Magazine*, 1893.
4/- Second Prize: Bound Volume *McEwan's Shorthand Notes & Queries*.
1/6 Third Prize: *Humours of Shorthand.*

For the neatest and most correct transcription of passage given below.

EXAMINATION PAPER No. 4.

How difficult it is to account for the awe with which we see a spirit.

It is an important improvement, which I think I might do well to adopt.

Each, all, may, in, or, other, our, without.

Write the above neatly in Shorthand, and send to the Editor, with Examination Fee of Threepence.

All Non-Prize-Winners who receive 90 per cent. marks will be presented with the following Certificate of Merit:—

"THE YOUNG PHONOGRAPHER."

CERTIFICATE.

Awarded to ....

who possesses an accurate knowledge of Grammalogues.

OLIVER McEWAN, *Editor*.

March, 1894.
Registered No...........

NOTE.—Every Paper must be Witnessed, the witness writing and signing the following declaration:—" Written in my presence, without assistance or reference to books.

THE

Young Phonographer,

— AND —

SHORTHAND BEGINNER'S MAGAZINE.

EDITED BY OLIVER McEWAN,

EDITOR "McEWAN'S PHONOGRAPHIC MAGAZINE," "THE SHORTHAND CRITIC AND REVIEW," AND "SHORTHAND NOTES AND QUERIES."

No. 6. VOL. I.] APRIL, 1894. [Price 1d.. 1/6 per annum, post free.

CONTENTS.

THE

SCHOOLDAYS OF SHERLOCK

WITH HIS FRIENDS,

TOM, DICK, AND HARRY.

BY O. McEWAN.

CHAPTER I.—THE BROKEN WINDOW.

ONE

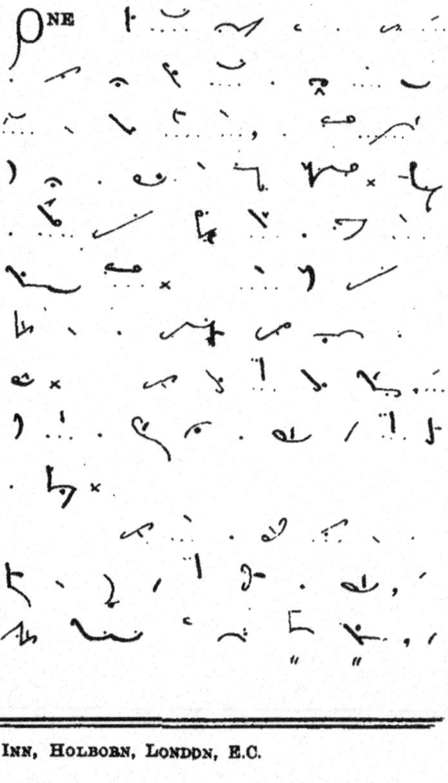

Editorial Office 4, FURNIVALS INN, HOLBORN, LONDON, E.C.

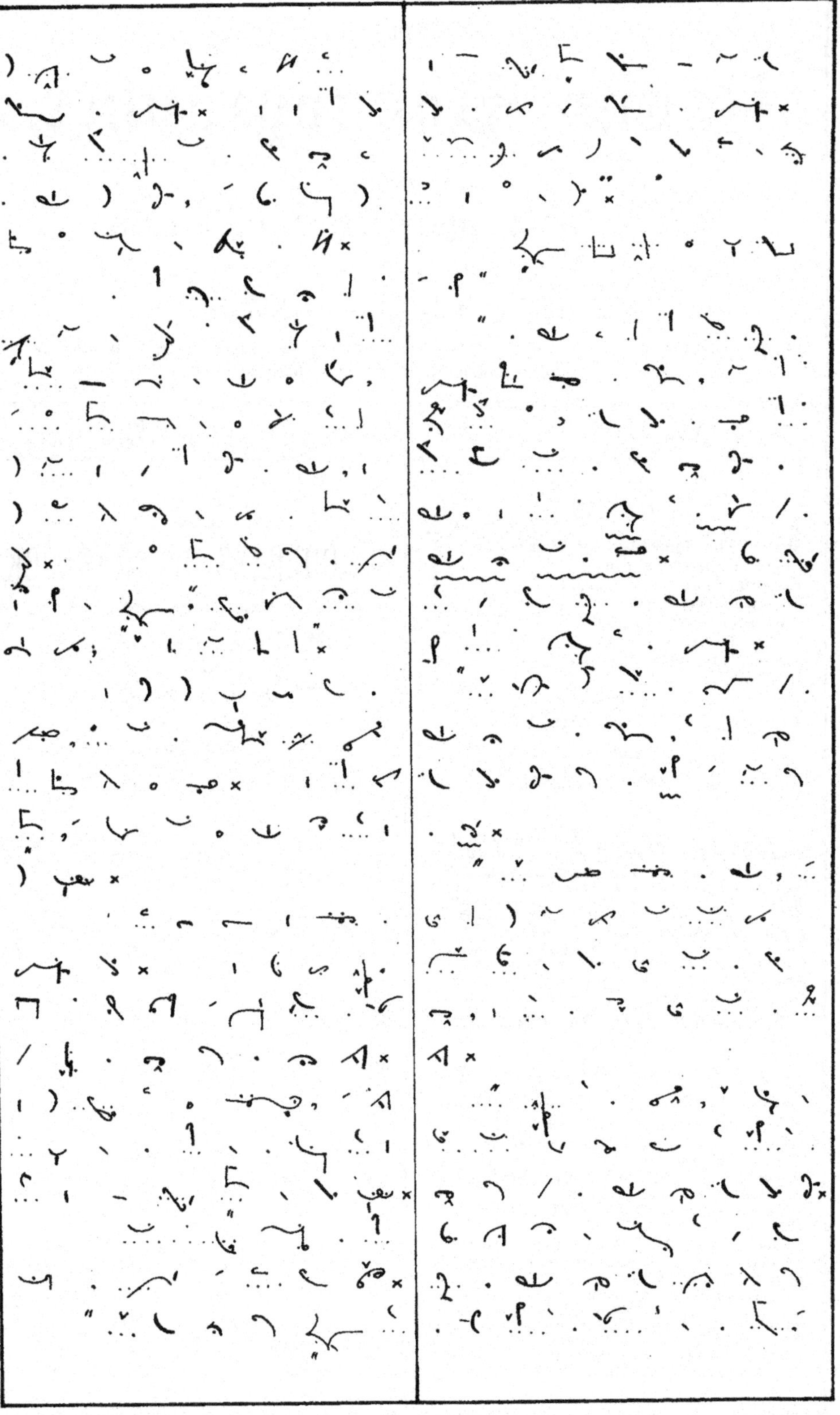

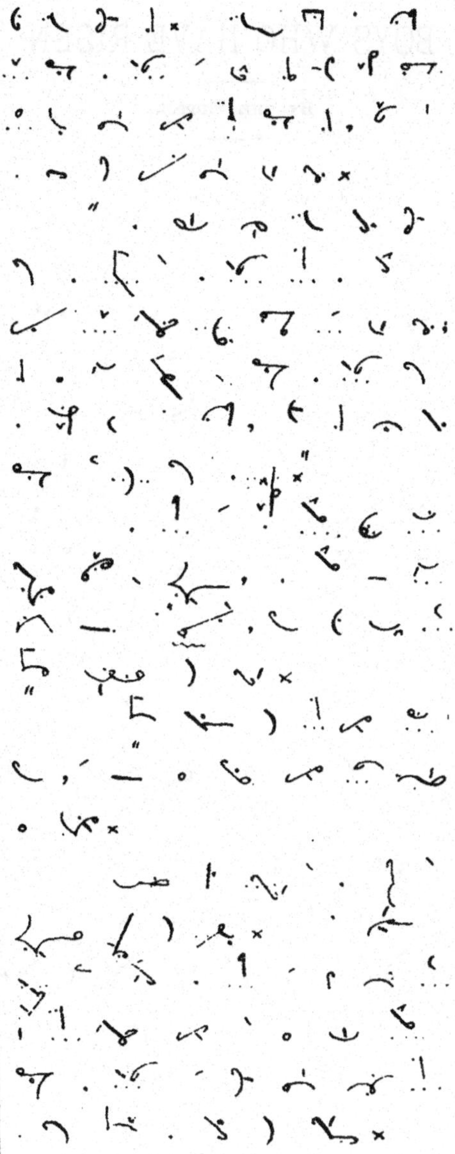

(To be continued.)

Contents of April

Shorthand Notes and Queries.

1. Speech by the Prince of Wales.
2. Story by Lady Susan Keppel.
3. Special Articles by O. McEwan.

12 Pages. Price Twopence.

JOHN HEYWOOD, PUBLISHER.

FACTS IN NATURAL HISTORY.

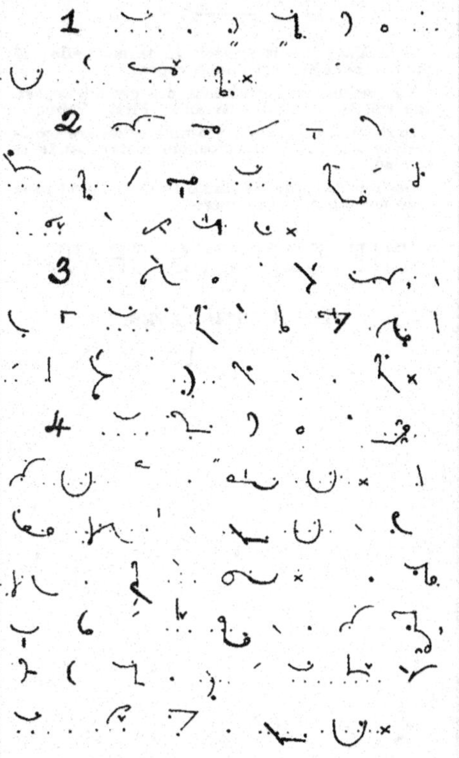

"Shorthand Notes and Queries,"

(April Number Now Ready),

FOR SECOND GRADE LEARNERS.

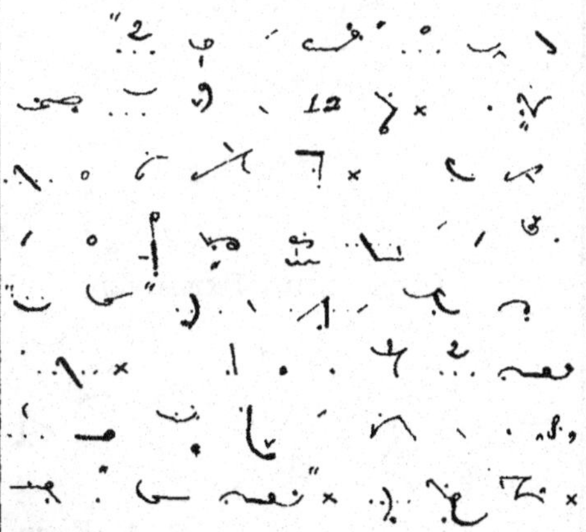

IMPORTANT.

INSTRUCTIONS FOR READING THIS MAGAZINE.

This Magazine is written in three grades of the Learner's Style of Phonography.

All outlines *not vocalised* are *grammalogues*, and will be found in Pitman's "First" Primer.

In the first story many grammalogues are vocalised, so as to enable the most elementary students to read it.

Begin to read the Magazine from the *first* page—do not *dip* here and there.

THE EDITOR'S CHAT.

THE CERTIFICATES.

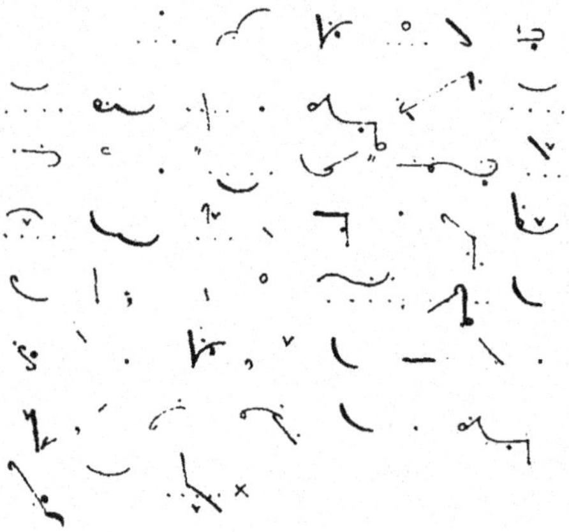

"COPY."

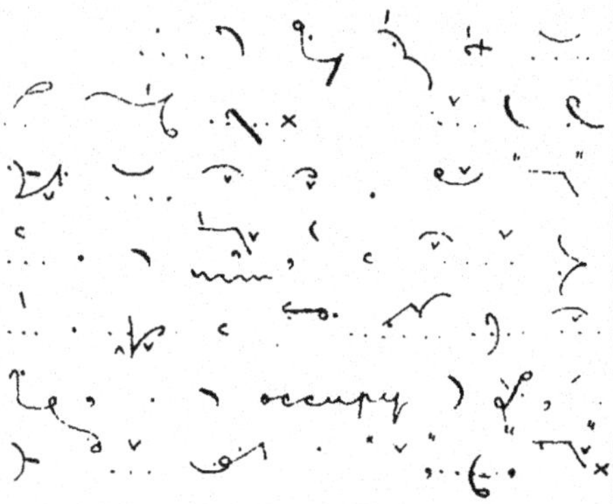

DIFFICULTIES EXPLAINED.

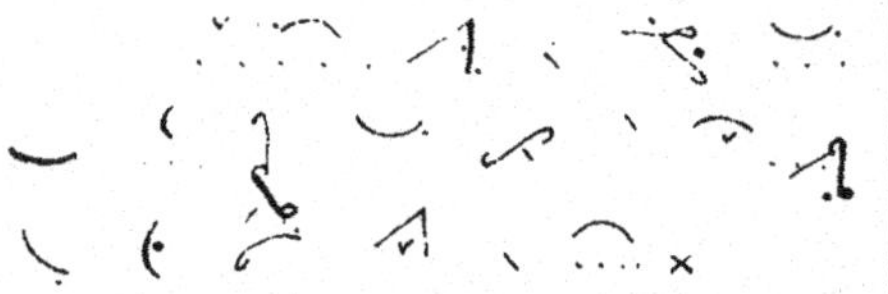

O. McEwan.

BOYS WHO HAVE RISEN

By the Editor.

TOM SMITH.

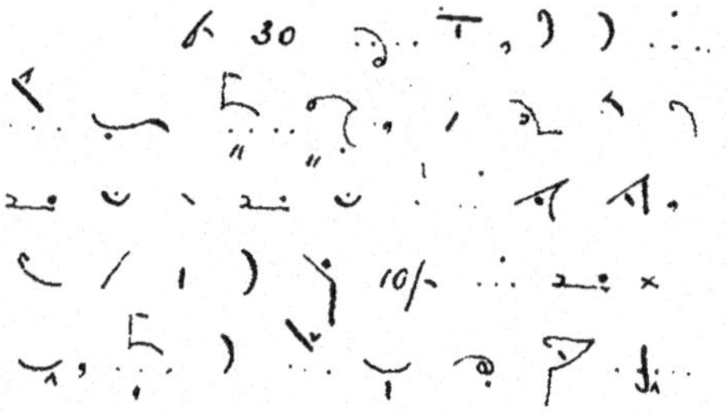

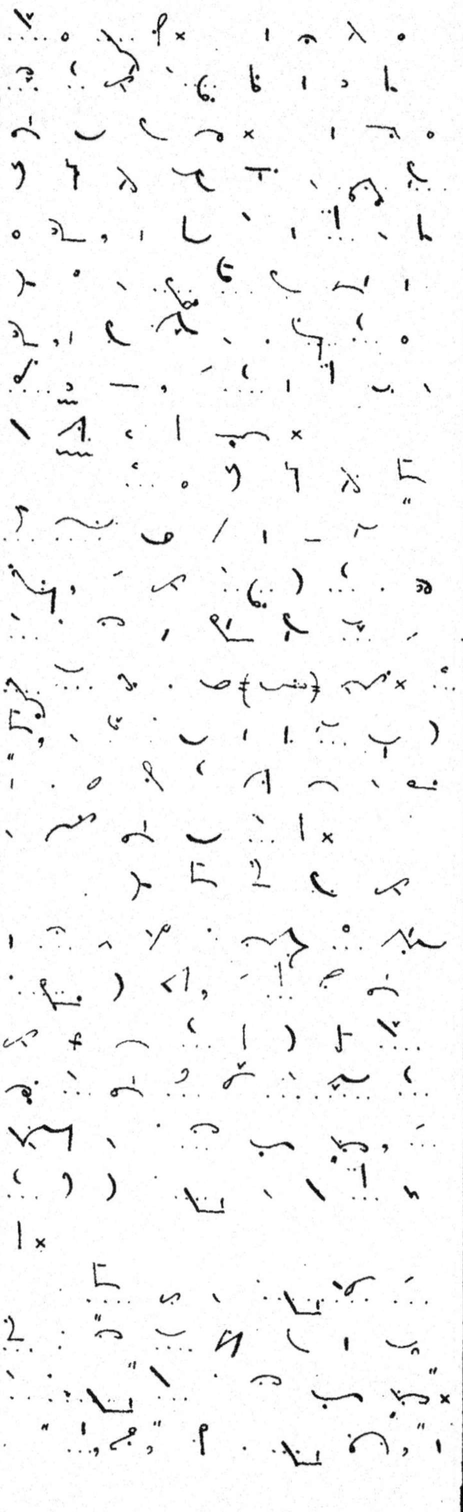

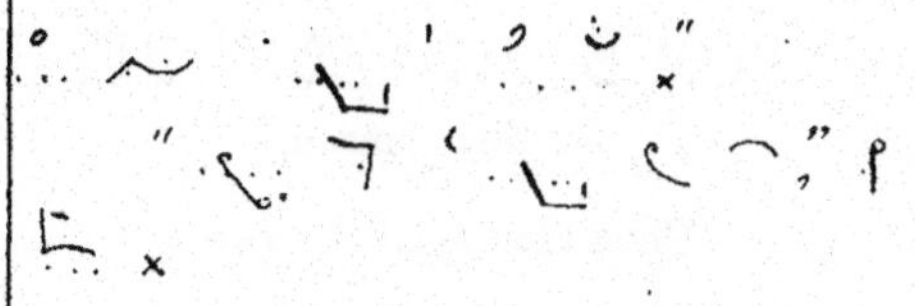

(To be concluded next month).

A COMMON ERROR.

LOOKED = LOOKT.

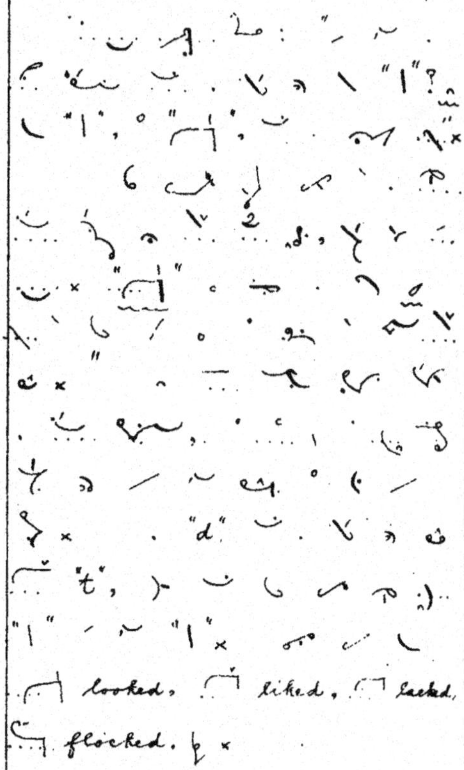

To Teachers, Secretaries of S.W.A.'s, &c.—

"Young Phonographer"

at Trade Price.

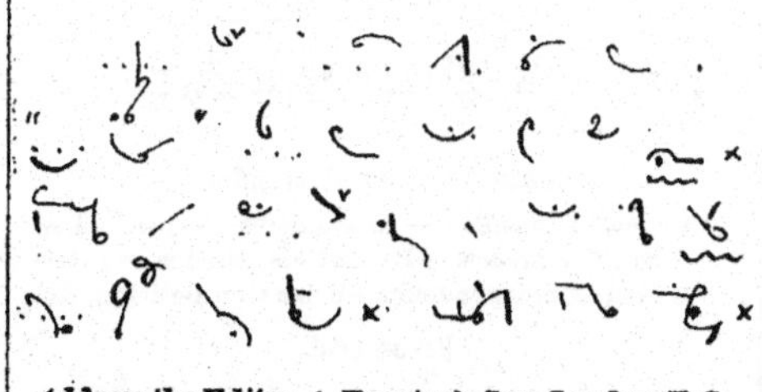

Address the Editor, 4, Furnivals Inn, London, E.C.

TOM'S ADVENTURE.

By the Editor.

Chapter III.—Saved.

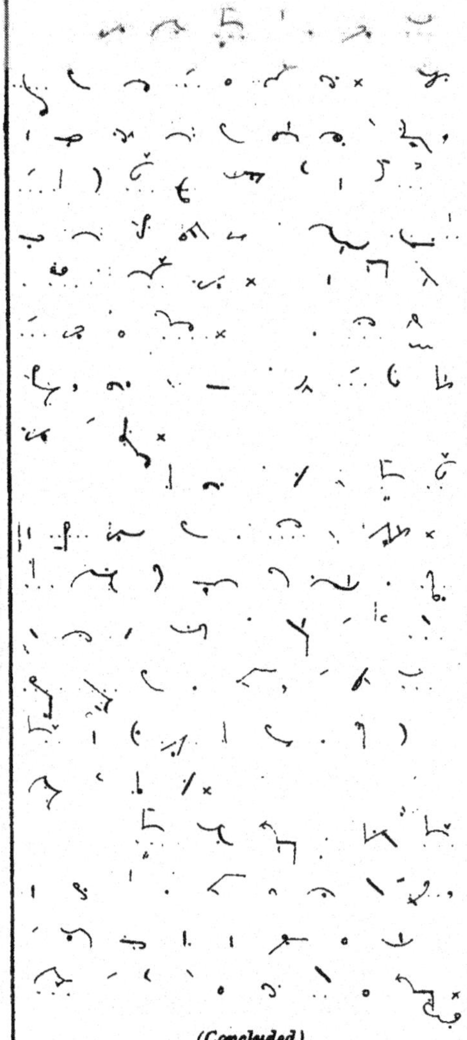

(Concluded).

LEARN THEM.

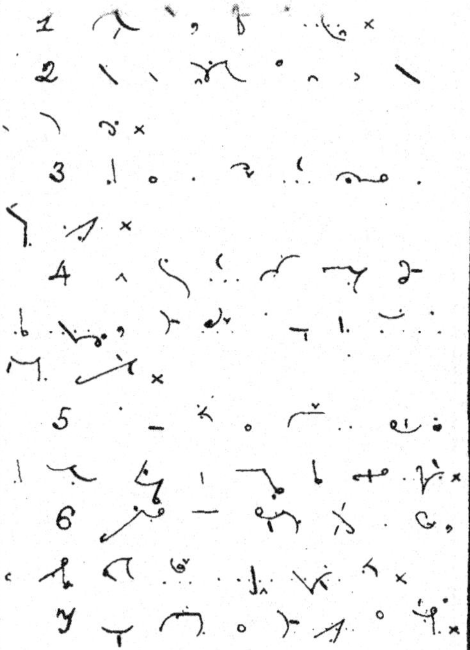

Little Smiles.

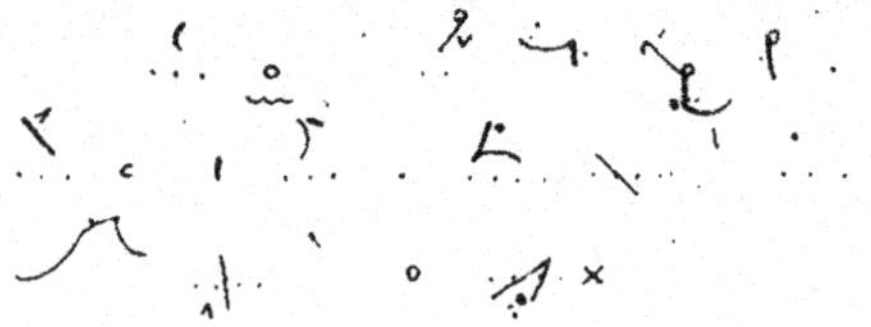

He did not Pay his Respects.

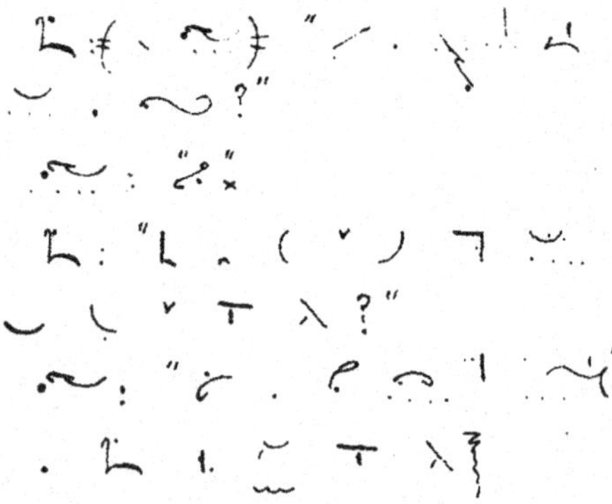

RESULT OF "THE YOUNG PHONOGRAPHER" COMPETITION No. 4.

FIRST PRIZE: Wm. Rutherford, Dosthill, Tamworth.
SECOND PRIZE: G. L. A. Lewis, 6, Dawson Street, Dublin.
THIRD PRIZE: A. Jones, Tyne Villa, Bembridge, Isle of Wight.
FOURTH PRIZE: F. Pate, 9, Grimshawe Street, Burnley.

Honours, 100: The Lady Mary Keppel, W. B. Duck, G. Drinkwater, Alma E. Hunt, Harriet Watson, H. Edwards, E. Sharp, W. J. Gear, M. H. Jackson, C. H. Donne, D. Campbell, C. Walker, J. J. Robinson, J. Grieves, W. R. Kindmarsh, L. F. Warner, Frances J. Barker, Hilda Watson, A. M. Hadfield, Gertrude Bramham, J. H. Pym, R. Campbell, W. E. Agnew, H. Parker, S. Bushell, T. B. Webster, J. Watson, J. Hetherington, T. Inglis, G. H. Clarke, E. Moors, Annie J. Watkin, F. J. Gordge, A. Moss, T. Heywood, T. Fletcher, T. W. Hall, E. A. Jarrett, W. Horton, E. Hawkins, J. R. Foster, P. A. Holdroyd, J. Gascoigne, H. Cogger, A. Dillingham, E. Richards, J. A. Brome, J. Cunningham, R. H. Ingram, E. Haines, Louie Johnson, W. H. Wardel, W. H. Bond, P. B. Hancock, P. A. Knott, W. J. Gill, W. Watson, J. C. Cole, J. W. Oldfield, J. Sykes, A. E. Weech, G. F. Barling, A. Holland, F. J. Doman, W. McPherson, H. P. Joinson, R. Kershaw, H. Baildom, P. Child, Sarah E. Geeson, W. Towell, H. Sharpe, S. Kirk, W. A. B. Briggs, E. J. Tansley, A. W. Cox, J. J. Clarke, T. Moors, J. E. Errington, F. J. P. Buckland, H. Abbott, P. Hanglin, J. Ranson, L. Argles, A. Nowers, T. Gibson, F. Heckford, A. O. Harpur, H. Barnden, A. E. Knight, E. R. Abbott, G. Pamely, W. Banham, A. Brookes, H. Sharpe, J. Westmoreland, James Westmoreland, J. E. Bayley, T. W. Elliott, G. W. Anderson, R. F. Baggett, H. F. Gordon, A. Cole, W. Willington, S. Drinkwater, E. J. Towler, W. H. Stanley, W. J. D. Mutch, E. R. Lee, H. Shawcroft, J. Leitch, J. Spreight, A. H. Tatum, Annie M. Smith, W. Edwards, A. Freeman, L. Kate Porter, S. E. Lovatt, H. M. Thompson, J. E. Ballard, J. W. Deanes, E. J. Mansfield, W. J. Green, H. Parfitt, C. H. Watkins, Mary E. Kickard, G. L. G. Simmons.

95 Marks: L. Franklin, O. Mills, F. G. Pearce, T. Simpson, J. F. Walker, C. Delabene Marsden.

"THE YOUNG PHONOGRAPHER" EXAMINATIONS

FOR CERTIFICATES OF MERIT.

Dec., 1893.	Neatness.*	June, 1894.	Advanced Vocalisation.
Jan., 1894.	Vocalisation.*	July, "	Knowledge of Contractions.
Feb., "	Transcription.*	Aug., "	Simple Phrasing.
Mar., "	Knowledge of Grammalogues.*	Sept., "	Simple Exceptional Outlines.
April, "	Knowledge of Rule Numbers.	Oct., "	Business Phrases.
May, "	Knowledge of Advance Rules.	Nov. "	A Business Letter.

12 CERTIFICATES AND GRAND AWARD OF MERIT.

A Fee of 3d. is charged for each Examination (Grand Certificate free), or 2/-, if remitted on entering first Examination, is accepted in settlement of Examination Fees.

** Papers for this Exams. may still be sent in—Get Back Numbers.*

GRAND COMPETITIONS FOR YOUNG PHONOGRAPHERS.

12 EXAMINATIONS FOR 12 CERTIFICATES.

EXAMINATION No. 5.

Two Prizes of Bound Volumes of *McEwan's Shorthand Notes & Queries*, value 5/-,

For the neatest copy of the Shorthand on col. 1, page 4, of this issue, "Editor's Chat," and for giving the numbers of the *pages* or *paragraphs* in Pitman's Primers or "Instructor," in which are given the rules employed in all outlines for words of two syllables.

Examination Fee, 3d., must be remitted with Paper.

All Non-Prize-Winners who receive 90 per cent. marks will be presented with a Certificate of Merit.

NOTE.—Every Paper must be Witnessed, the witness writing and signing the following declaration:—"Written in my presence, without assistance or reference to books."

"Not Known" at Pitman's. Sole Publisher, JOHN HEYWOOD, 2, Amen Corner, London; and Deansgate, Manchester.

THE Young Phonographer,

— AND —

SHORTHAND BEGINNER'S MAGAZINE.

EDITED BY OLIVER McEWAN,

EDITOR "McEWAN'S PHONOGRAPHIC MAGAZINE," "THE SHORTHAND CRITIC AND REVIEW," AND "SHORTHAND NOTES AND QUERIES."

No. 7. VOL. I.] MAY, 1894. [Price 1d., 1/6 per annum, post free.

COMMENCED IN NUMBER 5—MARCH.

THE SCHOOLDAYS OF SHERLOCK

WITH HIS FRIENDS,

TOM, DICK, AND HARRY.

BY O. McEWAN.

CHAPTER II.—THE DOCTORS RING.

"SHERLOCK

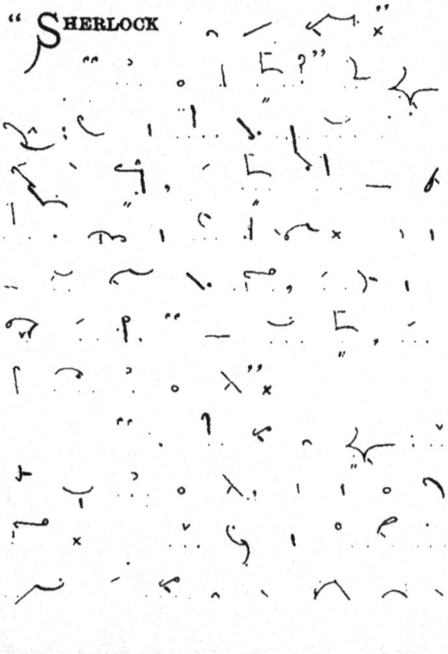

Published at 4, Furnivals Inn, London, by OLIVER McEWAN.

WHOLESALE AGENT: J. HEYWOOD, LONDON AND MANCHESTER.

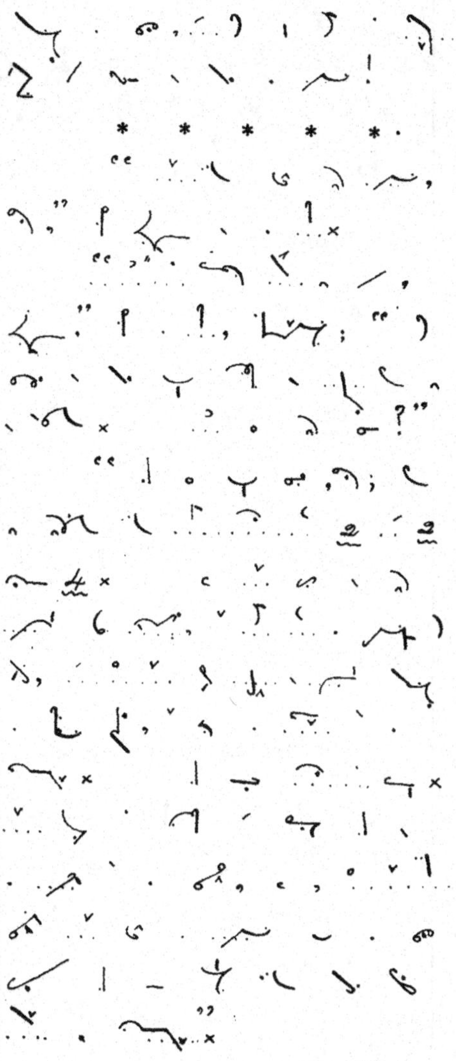

(To be continued.)

SCIENCE NOTES.

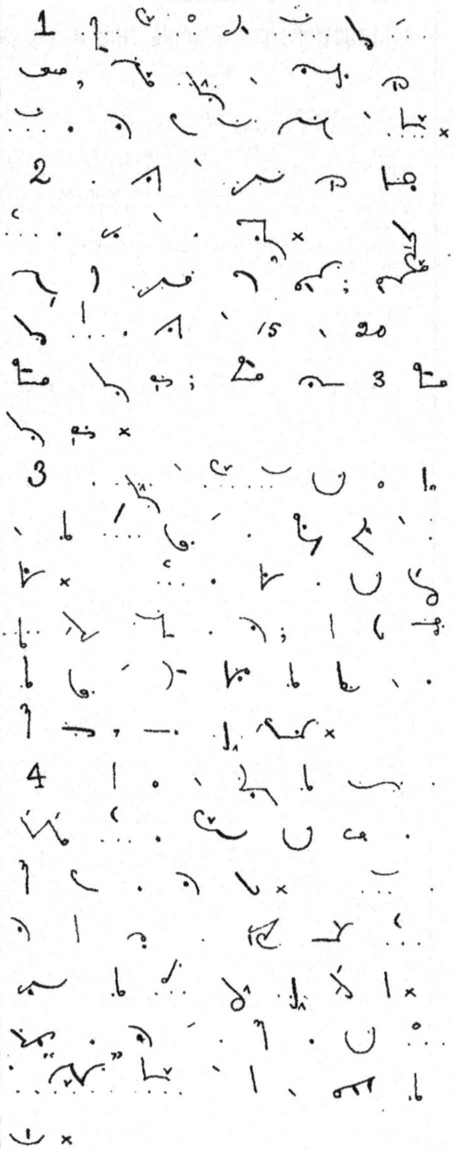

IMPORTANT.

INSTRUCTIONS FOR READING THIS MAGAZINE.

This Magazine is written in three grades of the Learner's Style of Phonography.

All outlines *not vocalised* are *grammalogues*, and will be found in Pitman's "First" Primer.

In the first story many grammalogues are vocalised, so as to enable the most elementary students to read it.

Begin to read the Magazine from the *first* page—do not *dip* here and there.

THE EDITOR'S CHAT.

"McEwan's Shorthand Weekly."

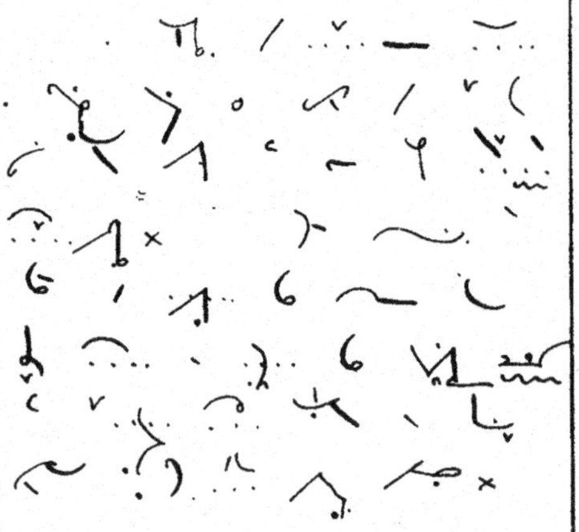

The New Weekly.

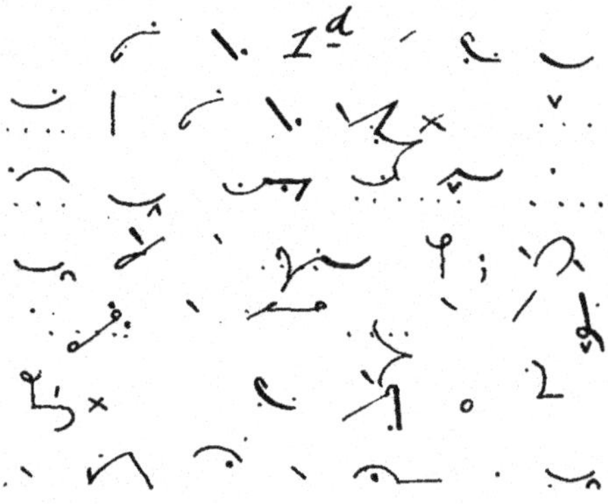

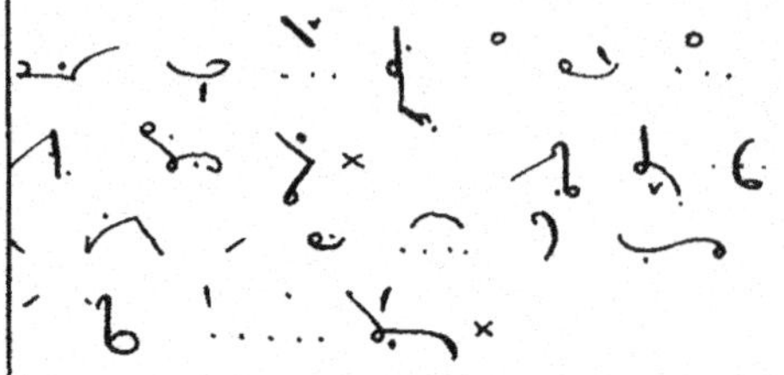

Comparisons are Odious.

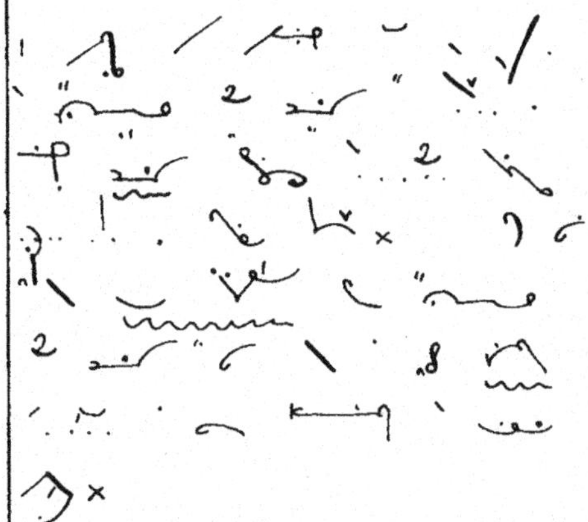

On the Editor's Return

Owing to the Editor's absence from town, the July papers have not been examined.

No Exam. this month.

LESSONS FROM AMUSING ERRORS.

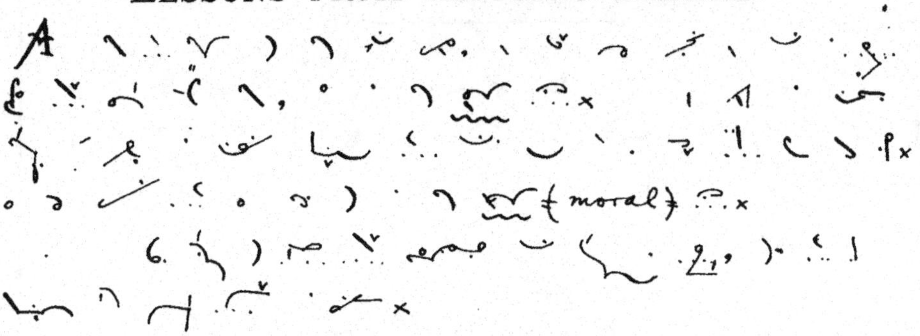

CRUELTY AND MORALITY.

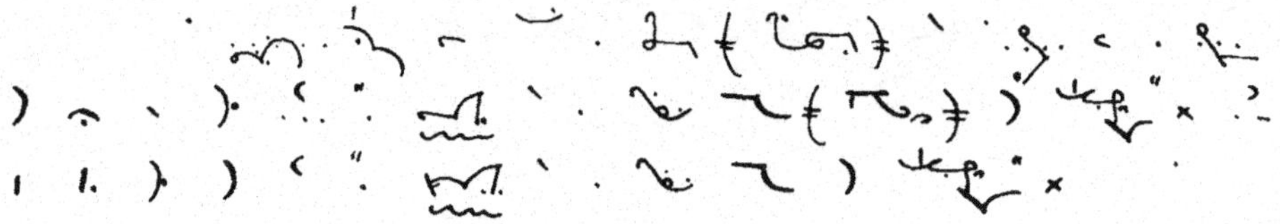

AMAZING AMUSEMENT.

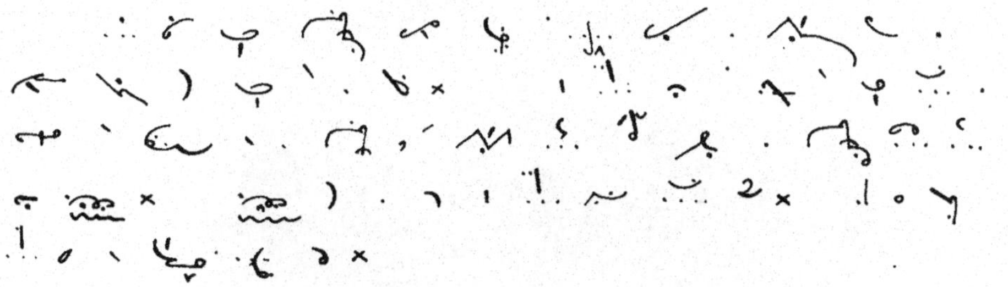

CATS!

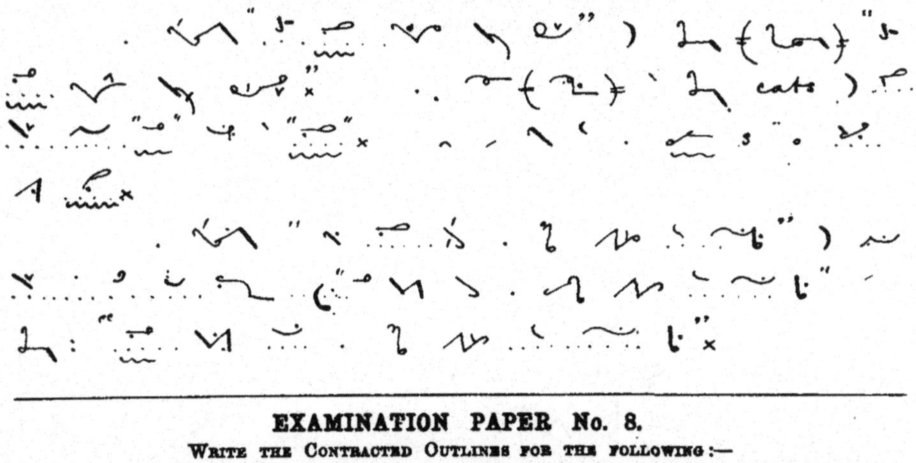

EXAMINATION PAPER No. 8.

WRITE THE CONTRACTED OUTLINES FOR THE FOLLOWING:—

Acknowledge, anything, Catholic, character, danger, difficulty, domestic, enlarge, especially, establish, expect, govern, immediately, influence, information, interest, irregular, regular, knowledge, magazine, manuscript, mistaken, never, next, object, peculiar, perform, phonographer, practice, probable, reform, represent, respect, satisfaction, subject, satisfactory, understand, yesterday.

☞ SEE NEXT PAGE.

"THE YOUNG PHONOGRAPHER'S" HOLIDAY.

EVIAN LES BAINS.

IMPORTANT NOTICES.

1.—"VERBATIM REPORTING" is almost ready, but cannot be delivered for some days after the 27th July.

2.—Owing to the prolonged illness of the Editor, the two other Magazines may not be ready till August 7th.

3.—All the Prizes in the "Grand Competition" are ready, and only require the Editor's signature to be sent out.

4.—Results of Competition next month.

G. NORTHDALE, *Sub-Editor.*

THE

Young Phonographer,

— AND —

SHORTHAND BEGINNER'S MAGAZINE.

EDITED BY OLIVER McEWAN,

EDITOR "McEWAN'S PHONOGRAPHIC MAGAZINE," "THE SHORTHAND CRITIC AND REVIEW," AND "SHORTHAND NOTES AND QUERIES."

No. 11. VOL. I.] SEPTEMBER, 1894. [Price 1d. 1/6 per annum, post free.

EXAMINATION No. 9. Examination Fee, 3d.

A "Perfection" Fountain Pen, value 10/6, will be awarded to the reader who sends in the best list of 50 Phrases in Shorthand on the model of those given in Pitman's Second Grade Book or "Manual," such as *I am, he was.* Preference will be given to lists which do not include any to be found in Pitman's lists.

EXAMINATION No. 10. Examination Fee, 3d.

A "Perfection" Fountain Pen, value 10/6, will be given for the best paper received containing the correct outlines for the following words:—Protestant, war, hymn, divorce, zion, pure, situation, crisis, poet, young, me, most, fallen, poorest, condition, pious, commotion, purist, partake.

Papers must be witnessed thus: "Written in my presence, without assistance or reference to books."
Signature of Witness.

RESULTS OF No. 8 EXAMINATION.

FIRST PRIZE: John H. Bell, 14, Thirlmere-road, Liverpool.

SECOND PRIZE: John J. Robinson, Harleigh Villa, Orrell-lane, Aintree.

HONOURS, Certificates (100 per cent.): Arthur H. Tatum, Lizzie Butler, Tom B. Webster, T. Moors, P. A. Knott, T. Inglis, J. W. Deanes, W. Rutherford, Annie M. Smith, W. E. Edwards, E. Moors, W. Mutch, Leslie Argles, S. Bushell, W. R. Hindmarsh, J. W. Hall, W. B. Duke, M. H. Jackson, W. Whiffin, Lilla K. Porter, G. Drinkwater, T. Johnstone, J. H. Stevenson, Alma E. Hunt, J. Grieves, W. Hardy, H. Dyson, J. Cowl, W. E. Agnew, H. Edwards, T. Squair, G. Race.

PASSES (90 per cent.): Gertrude G. Leggott, A. Cole, E. J. Fowler, J. G. Jenkinson, T. Heywood.

FURTHER RESULTS.

No. 7 Examination. Passes (90 per cent.): J. J. Branson, L. Price, S. Payne, R. J. Taylor, A. Moss, A. H. Tatum, C. H. James, G. Race.

No. 6 Examination. Passes (90 per cent.): E. J. Mansfield, A. W. Cocks, A. Moss, A. H. Tatum.

No. 5 Examination. Pass (90 per cent.): J. Branson.

No. 2 Examination: J. H. Pym.

EACH CHAPTER IS A COMPLETE STORY.

COMMENCED IN NUMBER 5—MARCH.

THE

SCHOOLDAYS OF SHERLOCK

WITH HIS FRIENDS,

TOM, DICK, AND HARRY.

BY O. McEWAN.

CHAPTER VI.—SOME CANDLE GREASE.

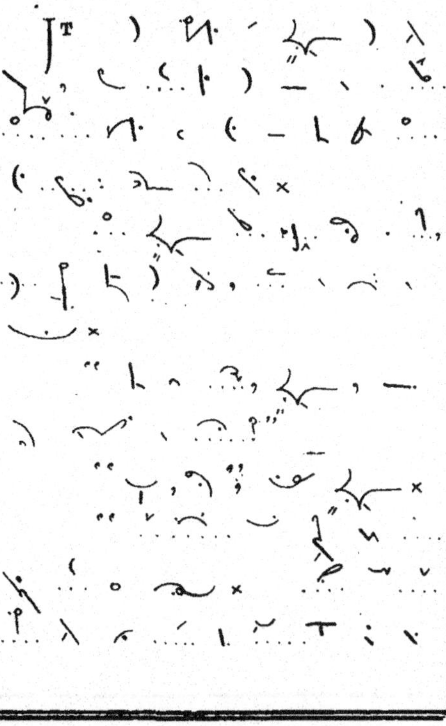

Published at The London Academy of Shorthand, 4, Furnivals Inn, London, by OLIVER McEWAN.
WHOLESALE AGENT: J. HEYWOOD, LONDON AND MANCHESTER

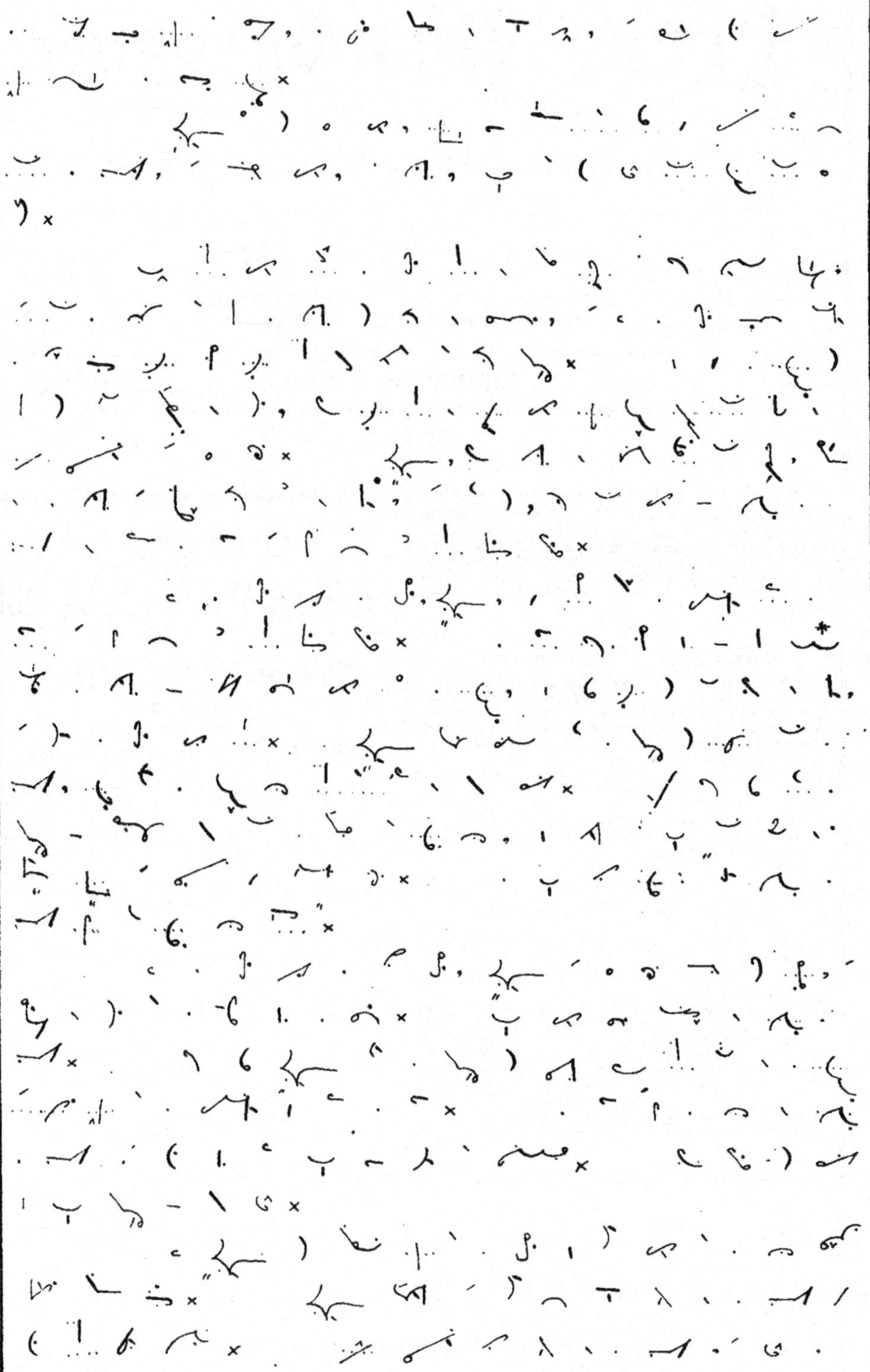

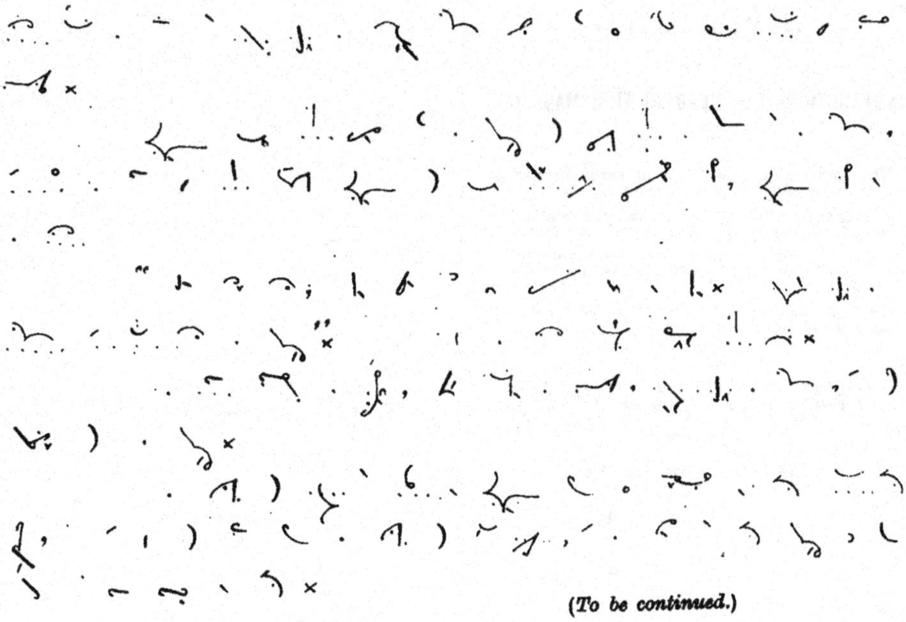

(To be continued.)

"McEWAN'S SHORTHAND WEEKLY."

Annual Subscription, 6/6; reduced to 5/6 if paid at once.

NOTICE.—All Subscriptions to *The Young Phonographer* are now completed. The two extra issues of the *Y.P.* FREE to those who NOW subscribe to the Weekly.

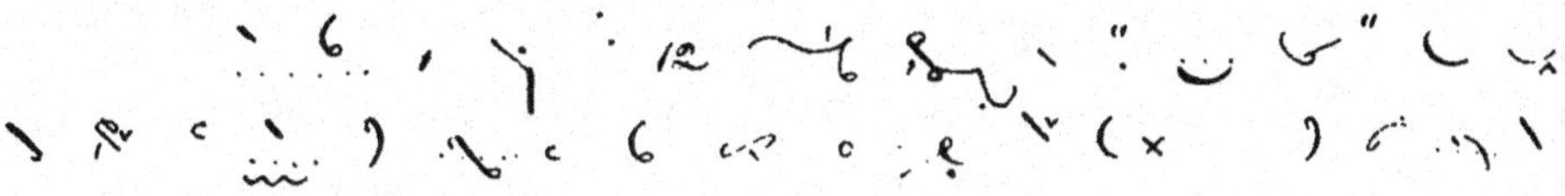

TWO EXTRA NUMBERS—NOVEMBER AND DECEMBER.

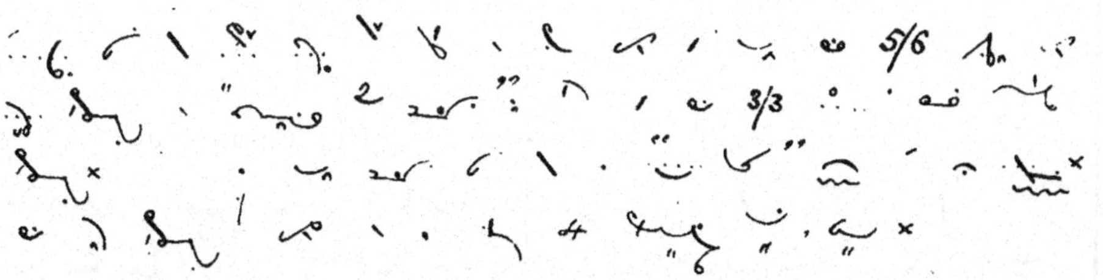

Send 6d. at once for sample copies of *Critic*, *Notes and Queries*, and the *Phonographic Magazine*, to the Editor, 4, Furnivals Inn, London, E.C.

IMPORTANT.

INSTRUCTIONS FOR READING THIS MAGAZINE.

This Magazine is written in three grades of the Learner's Style of Phonography.

All outlines *not vocalised* are *grammalogues*, and will be found in Pitman's "First" Primer.

In the first story many grammalogues are vocalised, so as to enable the most elementary students to read it.

Begin to read the Magazine from the *first* page—do not *dip* here and there.

THE EDITOR'S CHAT.

Getting up Speed.

"Verbatim Reporting."

The Grammalogues.

"In Darkest Phonography."

The Contractions.

THE DISTINCTION OF SIMILAR WORDS.

[shorthand]

PHRASING.

[shorthand]

1883

[shorthand]

INTERSECTIONS.

[shorthand]

"VERBATIM REPORTING."

[shorthand]

IS THE PRICE TOO MUCH?

[shorthand]

3/6

THE CERTIFICATES: SEND IN YOUR CLAIMS.

[shorthand]

48

10

O. McE.

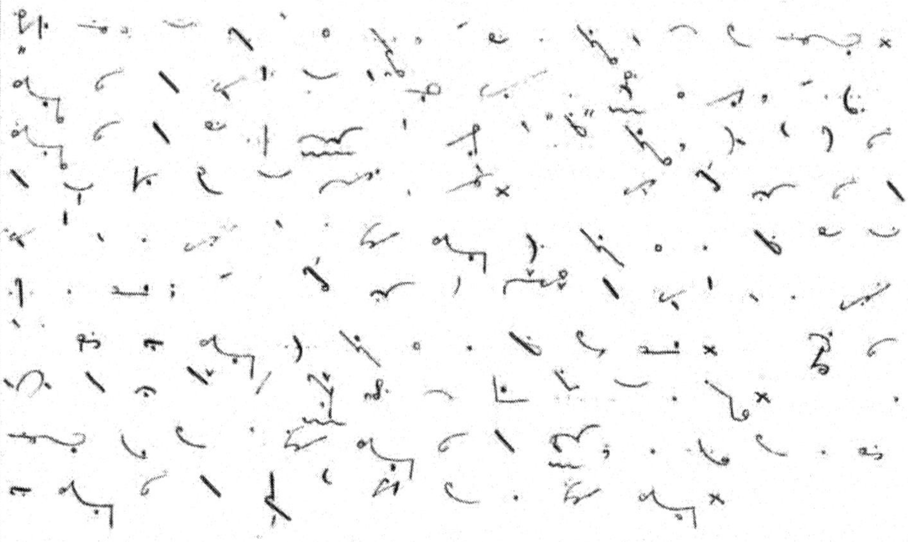

36 Fountain Pens.

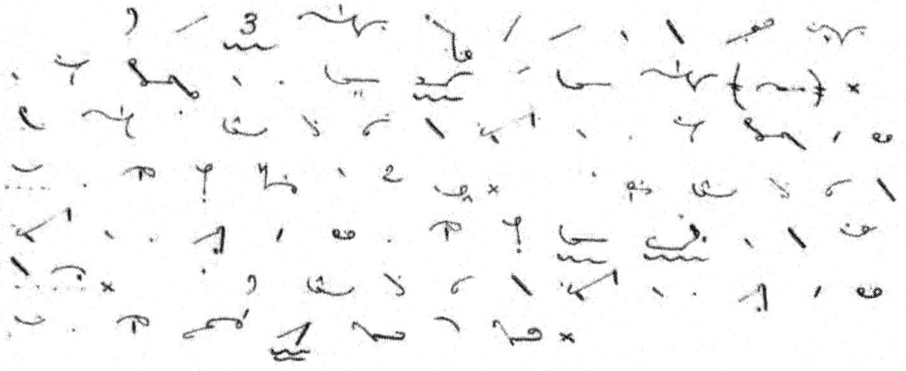

SEE NO. 1 "McEWAN'S PHONOGRAPHIC WEEKLY," READY DEC. 7TH.

NOTICE TO COMPETITORS.

The name of Prize Winner in No. 12 Examination will appear in No. 1 of *McEwan's Phonographic Weekly*. By the time this last issue of the *Y.P.* is in the hands of readers, every competitor will have been communicated with, and a Certificate awarded.

THE GOLD MEDAL FINAL COMPETITION,

For those who have passed the 12 Examinations. Particulars of this will be announced in No. 1 of *McEwan's Phonographic Weekly*.

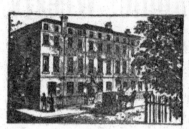

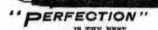

CPSIA information can be obtained
at www.ICGtesting.com
Printed in the USA
BVOW04*1809151017
497628BV00011B/48/P

9 781169 219564